I WAS THERE IN '66

I WAS THERE IN '66

Steve Batchelor

ATHENA PRESS
LONDON

I WAS THERE IN '66
Copyright © Steve Batchelor 2006

All Rights Reserved

ISBN 1 84401 668 4

First Published 2006 by
ATHENA PRESS
Queen's House, 2 Holly Road
Twickenham TW1 4EG
United Kingdom

Printed for Athena Press

ABOUT THE AUTHOR

Steve Batchelor is a fifty-six-year-old businessman, who is both an avid reader and a committed sports fan.

His only literary claim to fame to date is the publication of technical articles in various trade journals, but this is his first – and probably his only – book, and relates to a story that has now become a part of English sporting legend.

Steve lives in Northampton as a single parent with two of his three children, Paul aged, twenty-five, and Heather, aged seven.

DEDICATIONS

This book is dedicated to my late parents. For Dad, who gave me a love of sport, and for Mum, who gave me a love of life.

I could not have written this without the encouragement and support of my good friends Jayne and Therese, to whom I am eternally grateful. Thanks are also due to my eldest daughter, Emma, for always being so sensible.

Finally, to my many friends in the 'upper loft' among whom I have acquired the nickname of 'Bill' due to my propensity to quote from the bard, and to all Rangers supporters (not the Glasgow lot) for whom the expression 'oft expectations fail' is most appropriate. Thanks for your inspiration.

ABOUT THIS BOOK

This book is written from memory and is based on fact, the truth as I recall it and from notes I made at the time in my tournament programme. I apologise in advance for any errors, inaccuracies or exaggerations.

I have taken some literary licence with some of the actual quotations and conversations at the time and apologise if this causes any embarrassment to anyone who may recognise themselves.

PREFACE

When I was seventeen I saw England win the football World Cup. In fact, I saw every single game played at Wembley during the 1966 championships and still have match tickets and memorabilia from each match.

The significance of what I witnessed at such a tender age has only recently begun to dawn on me as England struggle to try and recapture those halcyon days and the ever-increasing media hype never fails to dredge up memories of 1966 at every subsequent international football tournament.

In writing this book, I have tried to recapture the mounting excitement felt by the whole nation as England progressed steadily towards the final, and then my experience of the final itself and the aftermath.

My view is one of an ordinary football supporter and reflects the tensions felt at each game and the witty and sometimes cruel chants and comments of the crowd.

I have also tried to recreate the era as a social history from a working/middle-class family perspective. The book includes workplace and kitchen table conversations and the humour of the age. It was only forty years ago but in those days there were no computers or colour television, no mobile telephones, dishwashers or speed cameras. Footballers were paid modest wages and lived relatively ordinary lives, yet the game was beginning to change, with the use of substitutes and the pass back to the goalkeeper rule still to be introduced.

I hope you enjoy the experience as you find yourself transported back to an age when English football really did rule the world!

CONTENTS

1 9 6 0 s E N G L A N D

A Working Lad

I gazed up in awe at the vast walls of Wembley Stadium as I walked briskly past on my way to my first job.

I was sixteen, it was the summer of 1965 and I had just been offered a position as office junior with a company that manufactured ventilation fittings and were located at the bottom of Wembley Trading Estate, close to the famous old stadium.

I have to admit that the close proximity of the stadium had influenced my decision to start my working career here, despite the miserly starting salary of just £7 per week, from which I had already agreed to pay my mother £3 for rent and food.

My work duties were hardly challenging; they included filing, photocopying and taking telephone messages for the sales staff.

I lived with my parents and brothers and sisters at the family home in Kenton, near Harrow, and travelled every day to work by walking a mile to Kingsbury station and taking the tube a short distance to Wembley Park, from where I walked another mile to South Way.

The last part of this journey took me within a few yards of the rear walls of Wembley stadium and I was compelled, every time I walked past, to gaze up and wonder at the excitement felt by so many as they witnessed the historic events that had unfolded inside this majestic arena.

World Cup Awareness

During 1965 the whole country had finally awoken to the fact that England were to host the football World Cup the following year, and each day when I passed on my journey to and from work, I dreamed of being amongst the spectators to witness England's quest for glory. I vowed then that I would save enough money to buy tickets, and scoured the media daily for news of ticket application procedures.

Football Fan

I had been a football fan from an early age when, as a six-year-old, my dad had taken me to watch the Batchelor 'family' team, Queen's Park Rangers.

I saw my first match in 1956, a 0–0 draw against Norwich at Loftus Road and still remember parts of it to this day. Originally from Kilburn and Kensal Rise QPR were the natural team for us all to support and had been so since the 1930s.

As many as twenty-five members of my family have attended Queen's Park Rangers games at various times, and I am pleased to say that many still do.

Limited Ability

Although we attended every QPR home match, my father also regularly took me to see Chelsea to watch Jimmy Greaves, and to Fulham to watch Johnny Haynes play. I am sure he harboured ambitions for his son to enter the football profession. Unfortunately, my own subsequent footballing prowess was restricted to Wormwood Scrubs playing fields and similar north-west London venues, where during a twenty-year 'career' I turned out for a variety of inauspicious Sunday morning pub sides. However, I continued to harbour a love of 'the beautiful game'.

England Fan

As a young boy, living close to Wembley I had been to England schoolboy matches at the national football stadium. I saw my first full international on 23 October 1963, when, as part of the Football Association centenary year celebrations, I witnessed England take on the 'Rest of the World' team and win 2–1 in front of a full house of 100,000.

My ticket, which I still possess to this day, was expensive at the time, at 7s. 6d. and afforded me a position in the west standing enclosure, entrance 57 at turnstile H, and I felt eternal gratitude to my dad for providing me with this experience.

Although the match was played on a Wednesday, the kick-off time was set at 2.45 p.m. to enable the game to finish before it began to get dark; I never did understand why it could not be played under floodlights. Still, all I cared about was seeing the world's best players in action.

I was fourteen years old at the time and was enthralled by the skills of Eusebio and Di Stefano and the athleticism of Lev Yashin, the Russian goalkeeper, who had a fantastic game for the 'Rest of the World' team, despite being on the losing side in what, on reflection, was a largely uncompetitive exhibition match.

For me, at the time, it was a thrilling match packed with showmanship and skill, and I vividly remember Jimmy Greaves scoring the decisive second goal for England.

I then felt the rising excitement of the crowd as, despite a late flourish from the opposition, we held on to win.

England's Destiny

Using schoolboy logic I reasoned that if England had just beaten a team comprising of many of the best players in the world, they must surely be the best team in the world and were, therefore, certain to win the next World Cup, especially as the tournament was being held in England.

From this moment, I aspired to obtain tickets for the next tournament in order to support England at every possible match. I especially wanted to be there 'on the day', as I firmly believed it was England's destiny to become World Champions.

Social History

In those days there was only black and white television with a limited choice of two channels – ITV or BBC. The only football show was the BBC's *Match of the Day* at 10 p.m. on a Saturday night or the annual live FA Cup Final.

There were no computers, of course, and our home certainly did not possess any of the modern household appliances that are taken for granted today.

Brown and Mild

There were no big retail parks with gigantic supermarkets or fast food outlets; beer was bitter and usually either Watney's Red Barrel or Double Diamond, which had recently been increased to 1s. 8d. (almost 9p in modern currency) a pint. Mild was more popular than lager.

The Government of the day was drawn from Harold Wilson's Labour Party, who had taken power following a close election in 1963, from Harold Macmillan's 'You've never had it so good' era of Conservatism. In those times the trade unions were still influential over a lot of Labour Party policies and First Secretary of State, George Brown's, famous quote of 'Brothers, we are on our way' summed up the optimistic mood of the nation twenty years after the end of the Second World War.

Unhealthy Economy

Although inflation was rising fast and interest rates were comparatively high, it was felt by most ordinary people that the country was in pretty good shape, and very few citizens were disappointed by Charles de Gaulle's continuing obstinacy at refusing to consider UK entry into the new Common Market (EU), which seemed to be a very anti-British club at the time.

Credit Where it's Due

During the year, Barclay's Bank introduced the first ever British credit card, and few people realised the profound effect this was to have on everyone's lives in the years ahead.

My own father, who was an astute man, was dead set against the whole concept of conning people into borrowing money to buy goods 'on tick' and steadfastly refused to own a credit card. 'If I haven't got the money, we'll have to go without' was a common expression of his, which was reflected by many of his generation. However, despite his misgivings, it was not too long before all his offspring, including myself, were proud possessors of our own credit cards.

Top of the Pops

British pop music was dominant worldwide, especially in the USA. *The Beatles* and *Rolling Stones* were in their heyday and new bands such as *Pink Floyd* were just evolving.

As a teenager you were encouraged by the media to decide if you were 'a Beatle' or 'a Stone', as the popular misconception of the day was that they represented opposite ends of the social spectrum. *The Beatles*, allegedly, were the nice guys that any girl could take home to their mum with their smart suits and cute haircuts, and the *Rolling Stones*, were the scruffy, unwashed, swearing, drug-taking louts that no decent person could associate with. This seems utterly ridiculous looking back on it today, but was certainly the attitude permeated at the time.

As I considered myself a bit of a rebel, I was a Stones fan and even declined tickets to see *The Beatles* on one occasion as they were not cool enough for me. (Yes, it was a decision I regretted in subsequent years.) However, I did manage to see the *Rolling Stones* many times.

World News

Elsewhere in the world the USA were in the midst of a war in Vietnam and Australia had just started to send troops in support. Britain had refused to become involved militarily.

The anti-war movement was in its infancy in the UK, but news of its development in the United States was beginning to drift into our consciousness, particularly amongst young people of my age, who often speculated that if the British Government was to change its stance and offer to send troops as well they might consider conscripting people of my generation.

All over the world there seemed to be strife, with Russia jailing prominent writers as dissidents; India and Pakistan in conflict over Kashmir; and Mao Tse-tung, the Chairman of the Communist People's Republic of China declaring that 'Political power grows out of the barrel of a gun'.

England Swings

Men were starting to grow their hair longer as pop stars set the trends for millions to follow; sure enough, I stopped getting my hair cut when Jennifer at work described Mick Jagger as the sexiest man on the planet. Somehow, I thought by copying his hairstyle I would become more attractive to her; sadly, my ploy didn't work!

Meanwhile, Britain was gripped in a fashion revolution that had propelled 'Swinging England' – London in particular – to global attention, with fashion icons such as Mary Quant and Twiggy attaining international stardom.

Living in London as a teenager at this time I felt this was surely the best place on earth to live.

Football Tradition

English football too was envied all over the world through its honest sweat and endeavour, although it was the widely held belief that 'the continentals' were developing better individual skills. This was graphically illustrated when the Hungarians thrashed England 6–3 in their worst ever Wembley defeat in 1953 with the outstanding skills and swift inter-passing of Puskas, who scored twice, and Hidegkuti, who scored a hat-trick, completely bemusing the English defenders.

Two–Three–Five

The traditional team line-up of two full-backs, three midfielders and five forwards was also being radically changed following the different formations adopted, initially, by the Hungarians and South Americans. The original system, which had been developed in England almost one hundred years previously, was composed of a goalkeeper, two full-backs, three half-backs (midfielders) and five forwards: two wingers, two inside forwards and a centre forward.

Every match programme at this time set out teams in this manner, including the 1966 World Cup publication.

It'll Never Catch On

New formations such as 4–4–2 and 4–3–3 put far greater emphasis on defending and used overlapping full-backs and midfielders to break quickly to support the fewer forward players, who had started to develop techniques for holding the ball up, rather than automatically going straight for the goal.

Despite outrage from the football diehards and old English establishment that these newfangled ideas would never catch on, many astute coaches were watching these developments with interest and gradually trying to introduce them into the English game. There were few managers as aware, at the time, as Alf Ramsey. Interestingly, Ramsey had been playing as full-back on that humiliating Wednesday night in November 1953, when English football had been exposed by the sheer skill and speed of the Hungarians; he had even converted a late penalty to give the scoreline greater respectability.

It seems certain that Ramsey must have taken lessons from that game, and he often commented that English football must learn to play more like the continentals in order to develop.

It seems staggering now, but at the time of the Hungary match, English players used to take straight to the pitch a few minutes prior to kick-off; the fans were amused to see the Hungarians undertake a thorough 'warming up' routine for fifteen minutes before the start of the game.

After that result, it was not long before the pre-match warm-up became a regular part of the British game at every level.

Ramsey also noticed that teams did not need to have a 6' 3" battering ram centre forward to open up defences. Although Ramsey often featured Tottenham's Bobby Smith, who scored regularly for England, Smith was destined to become the last of the old-style, traditional English centre forwards, and paved the way for the more versatile, hard-running but highly-skilled and intelligent forward players such as Geoff Hurst and Roger Hunt.

RAMSEY'S INFLUENCE

Liverpool were emerging as the future dominant team in Europe, and with even QPR developing as possible Division Three championship contenders, my confidence approaching the World Cup was extremely high.

Ramsey Takes Charge

English international football was going through a renaissance following a disappointing exit from the 1962 World Cup final in Chile. The England manager at the time was Walter Winterbottom, but amazingly he did not get to pick the team. Instead, this was done by the English FA Committee.

The FA decided that Alf Ramsey was the man they wanted to take over due to his incredible achievement in raising humble Ipswich Town from the old Third Division to become League Division One champions and a recognised force in English football, with several new international players.

This followed a distinguished playing career for Ramsey, in which he had played thirty-two times for his country.

The FA Committee were shocked when Ramsey told them he must have sole jurisdiction over team selection and that he insisted on honouring the last three months of his Ipswich contract. This meant that for the last four matches of 1962, Winterbottom was asked to resume temporary control. His final match in charge was a 4–0 win over Wales, watched by a paltry 27,500 at Wembley.

A Bad Start

Ramsey's baptism in international football was an abject disaster; losing 5–2 to France in Paris in a European Nations Cup qualifier, his immediate response was to make five changes for his next match, including dropping Ron Springett as goalkeeper.

Scottish Grit

Ramsey bought in Leicester City's Gordon Banks for his debut against Scotland at Wembley. During this match, the Scottish defender Eric Caldow broke his leg and Scotland were reduced to ten men yet still finished up as 2–1 winners, although Banks was not culpable for either of the goals.

Gradual Improvement

After drawing 1–1 against Brazil in a friendly as part of their centenary celebrations, England then embarked on a six-match winning run, starting with a 4–2 win in Bratislava against Czechoslovakia, which marked a debut for winger Terry Paine and also heralded Bobby Moore's first match as captain.

They rattled up some huge scores, including an 8–1 win against Switzerland with a Bobby Charlton hat-trick and an 8–3 win against Northern Ireland in a match that saw Terry Paine's hat-trick overshadowed by Jimmy Greaves netting four times. This winning streak also included the memorable match against the 'Rest of the World'.

Auld Enemy Trilogy

However, England were again overcome by Scotland at Hampden Park, losing 1–0 in April 1964, watched by a record crowd of 133,245, which far exceeded ground safety levels. Scotland were full of confidence, winning their third successive match against the 'auld enemy', and played by far the better football with the controlled passing of their elegant midfielder, Jim Baxter, proving a perfect ally for the quicksilver runs of Dennis Law and backed up by some tigerish tackling from their highly motivated defenders.

England were simply overrun and outplayed, and already there were rumblings of discontent about Ramsey's choice of workmanlike players against those with flair.

Teambuilding

Ramsey was undeterred and England proceeded to win four successive games, including an interesting home friendly against Uruguay 2–1, which marked the debut of George Cohen at right full-back. Cohen was replacing former captain, Jimmy Armfield, who had held this position with distinction for the previous four years but was suffering from a long-term groin injury and was now also approaching the latter stages of his career. Cohen was a full-back with strength and pace who liked to join in the attack and conformed perfectly to Ramsey's strategies, as his overlapping runs and crossing ability obviated the need for a conventional winger. He was also a very good team player and was prepared to comply strictly with Ramsey's instructions. Cohen quickly established himself as the regular choice right back, and by the time the World Championships opened he had made this position his own.

This latest winning run also included a thrashing of the

United States 10–0 in New York in a match watched by a sparse crowd of just 5,000, mostly English expatriates. This time it was Roger Hunt's turn to score four times in a match, and the Liverpool forward began to make a name for himself as an accomplished goalscorer.

Lessons to be Learnt

However, England were brought back to earth with a bump again, performing disastrously in the Brazilian Centenary Tournament, where they failed to win at all, drawing 1–1 with Portugal and losing 1–0 to Argentina before being hammered 5–1 by Brazil in Rio. During this match, Pele and Garrincha completely destroyed England in a rampant second half after a fairly even first period had seen the sides go in level at one goal each.

Ramsey had experimented with Tony Waiters making his second appearance in goal, but he was promptly dropped in favour of Gordon Banks for subsequent matches.

Bend it Like Garrincha

Despite the tired performance of the English team, Ramsey felt lessons had been learnt and rather prophetically cited the examples of some stunning, swerving free-kicks against England as something they badly needed to learn to defend against better.

Second International

I saw my second England match at Wembley on Wednesday, November 18 1964, in a home international Championship match against Wales. Nottingham Forest centre forward Frank Wignall scored both of England's goals on his debut in a 2–1 win, but was to make only one other England appearance. This was a very makeshift England team with Tony Waiters having another run in goal, due to an injury to Gordon Banks, and only two of England's World Cup stars were present. The team selection was reflected in the relatively poor turnout of only 40,000 fans, who showed little enthusiasm for a mediocre match.

Tartan Tie

In April 1965, England finally stopped the rot against Scotland, drawing 2–2 at Wembley in a match that marked significant debuts for Nobby Stiles and Jackie Charlton, who were instrumental in keeping England in the game after injuries had reduced them to just nine fit players.

The Team Takes Shape

A series of inauspicious results followed as England struggled to develop a settled team throughout the rest of the year and they recorded their most impressive results in friendlies.

In May, they beat Hungary 1–0 at Wembley and a few days later drew 1–1 against Yugoslavia in Belgrade, which saw Alan Ball's first appearance in an England shirt where he immediately made an impact with his tireless running and bundling enthusiasm.

England Beat West Germany

In May they continued their progress by winning 1–0 against West Germany in Nuremberg, thanks to a Terry Paine goal in front of 70,000 fans.

However, they then struggled to beat Sweden 2–1, with a goal each for Alan Ball and John Connelly, before drawing a poor game with Wales in Cardiff 0–0.

Viennese Whirl

Tragically, England lost their next match by 3–2 to Austria at Wembley in what was my third appearance at a live England match and my only ever defeat.

Ron Springett was back in goal for this game and even I was vocal in my criticism, despite the fact that he was an ex-QPR keeper. With the World Cup looming, 65,000 spectators had turned up expecting to see another comfortable England win, but despite smartly taken goals from Bobby Charlton and John Connelly, defensive lapses enabled Austria to score three times and inflict an embarrassing defeat.

Winning Ways

Fortunately, England were back into winning ways when I saw my fourth match a month later as they beat Northern Ireland by 2–1, and in December, England recorded their best performance of the year when they defeated Spain in Madrid 2–0 with Bobby Charlton scoring in his sixtieth international.

The significance of the Spanish match was that it featured no less than nine of Ramsey's eventual World Cup winners and was the first time he did not include any recognised wingers in his team formation.

This performance, against the country that boasted Real Madrid as undoubtedly the finest club the world had ever seen and featured several of their players, was a milestone victory for Ramsey, who had finally convinced his critics that, on their day, England were capable of beating anybody.

EARLY 1966

Ticket Hopes

As the end of the year approached and attention turned towards future events in 1966, I was even more determined to gain tickets to see the impending World Cup and continued to scour the newspapers daily for details of the ticket availability in addition to writing directly to the FA and registering my name in advance with Wembley box office.

January 1966

The year had started with indifference from the population about the holding of the World Cup Association football finals. A mood of nonchalance seemed to prevail, with far more emphasis on the domestic season than on the impending World Championships.

Queen's Park Rangers were lying third in Division Three and challenging for promotion, and due to an outstanding youth policy, had produced no less than six England youth team players. With the signings of First Division veterans Les Allen and Jim Langley, they strung together an impressive winning run; but a poor start to the season had still left them a lot to do to make one of the top two places needed for promotion, as there was no such thing as play-offs in those days.

England Struggle

England started their international year early, on 5 January, when they met Poland in a friendly match played at Goodison Park, Everton, but failed to impress in a dull 1–1 draw.

Once again they were being written off. The workmanlike efforts of England's midfielders failed to create sufficient openings, and the absence of a recognised winger was again openly criticised.

February 1966

When ticket applications were announced, I duly applied for two tickets for all the Wembley matches – this was to be England's home base. I was delighted when the draw was made allocating all of England's group stage matches at this stadium.

I had decided that rather than face the embarrassment of not being successful in my quest for tickets, I would not tell anyone that I was applying and somehow managed to keep the secret from my family for several months.

England Beat West Germany – Again

I managed to get tickets to see England play a friendly against West Germany at Wembley on 23 February 1966. This was the first time I had a seat ticket at Wembley and I paid the vast amount of 25 s. (£1.25) for the privilege and went with a pal from work, Gerry, who had never seen an international match. 'I hope you get cushions at these prices,' he quipped.

'Why, are your farmers playing up?' I joked, but not being a Londoner this eluded him. Unfortunately, the high price of the seat ticket meant I couldn't afford a match programme, and this is the only one missing from my collection, which long ago passed the 1,000 mark for all the first-class matches I have attended.

Although England managed to win 1–0 with Nobby Stiles surprisingly scoring the winning goal, they failed to impress again. This game marked the first start in an England shirt for West Ham's Geoff Hurst, whose prolific goalscoring for the East London team had made it difficult to ignore him; however, in this match he had few opportunities. It was also debut day for full-back Keith Newton and a second appearance for Norman Hunter – neither player looked comfortable trying to adapt to the new playing system Ramsey was trying to introduce. I was just pleased to see an England win and, as I was still only sixteen at the time, I felt extremely mature being trusted to go to a night game.

Wingless Wonders

The press had now tagged England, with some irony, as Ramsey's 'wingless wonders', due to the new 4–4–2 team formation. I could not see how we could compete against the best teams in the world. Like most football fans, at the time I believed every team needed at least one winger capable of running at defenders and putting in crosses and I have to admit I also joined the bandwagon of questioning Ramsey's tactics.

20 March 1966

I awoke on this morning to read the terrible news that the Jules Rimet Trophy (The World Cup) had been stolen whilst on display at a stamp exhibition in London. The newspapers were speculating that the tournament would have to proceed without a trophy. In my imagination, I could picture Bobby Moore holding aloft an invisible cup – much like millions of schoolboys had done since tournaments were invented. The embarrassment to the FA, and the country as a whole, was acute, and the best Scotland Yard detectives were called in to investigate. The newspapers were merciless in their criticism of the poor organisation and lack of security, and FIFA, the world governing football body, were furious. The papers printed a plea for the cup to be returned, as this was a slight on the whole nation, whilst privately it was speculated this was the work of a Scotsman with a wicked sense of humour. The bizarre twist to the story was that exactly one week later the cup was discovered wrapped in newspaper in a south London suburban hedge. The finder was a black and white mongrel dog named Pickles, and the trophy was unceremoniously returned by the police to the FA to their immense relief. The dog's owner, Thames lighterman David Corbett, who was interviewed on the television newsreels, received a £3,000 cash reward; and his pet, who was on the front page of every newspaper, received an extra large bone!

Marsh Mania

QPR had signed a new inside forward from Fulham called Rodney Marsh who was rumoured to be very skilful but a bit of a troublemaker. I saw his first match, which was a 1–1 draw at Colchester, and was favourably impressed. A week later he made his home debut and became an instant hero, scoring twice in Rangers' 6–1 demolition of league leaders Millwall, whose fans tried to stage a sit-down protest on the pitch in an effort to get the game abandoned late in the second half. Sadly for me, QPR still just missed out on promotion, finishing in third place.

April 1966

Early in the month, England finally defeated Scotland 4–3 in a thrilling match at Hampden Park watched by a crowd of 123,052. The diminutive Scottish winger, Jimmy Johnson, had tormented the English defence but Alf Ramsey seemed to have instilled a strong team spirit into his England side and they competed resolutely and never seriously looked like being beaten. Ray Wilson missed the match through injury and his replacement, Keith Newton, struggled, but the strong running of the front pair – Geoff Hurst and Roger Hunt – was a constant threat and they were duly rewarded with Roger Hunt scoring twice and Geoff Hurst netting his first England goal.

Bobby Charlton had a huge influence in England's midfield, putting in a 'man of the match' performance and also registering on the score sheet.

Ticket Triumph

After what seemed an eternity, I finally received confirmation of my World Cup ticket order in a letter from the Football Association dated 12 April 1966, in which they advised me that my payment of £7. 18s. 6d. had been received and I was to be allocated two tickets for six matches in group A, grade three (standing only). I then waited impatiently for my actual tickets to turn up in the post.

End of Anxieties

Finally, after enduring agonies fantasising over the many different reasons my tickets to not show up – could have been lost or stolen – and cursing the postal service for their ineptitude, my set of precious tickets arrived. Despite enquiries from my mother about what the contents of the unobtrusive brown envelope might be, I secreted the tickets into my briefcase and there they stayed for the next few weeks.

My ticket application included all England's first-round matches, plus one other game in England's group between group rivals Uruguay, France or Mexico, plus the Wembley quarter-final and semi-final.

Ticket Secret

I now waited anxiously to see if my name would be pulled from the hat as a candidate to purchase tickets for the actual final.

As I had obtained my tickets in complete secrecy from my family, I could hardly contain my excitement at informing them I now had tickets for every match except the final and now eagerly waited for the tournament to begin.

May 1966

I purchased tickets to see England play Yugoslavia as they began their World Cup preparation in their final home match before the championships. An expectant crowd of 55,000 turned up expecting to witness another England goal fest.

Although they fielded a strong team, Jimmy Armfield, Norman Hunter and Bobby Tambling were destined not to appear in the World Cup matches; with Tambling being dropped permanently from the squad after just three internationals. Ramsey again tried a team with two wingers, this time Terry Paine and Tambling, but the 2–0 win was somewhat unconvincing. Yugoslavia had failed to qualify at

France's expense for the tournament due to their inability to beat lowly Norway and fielded a young and experimental side, yet were not overawed.

Redeeming Features

The two redeeming features of this untidy match were a promising debut by Martin Peters, who seemed to enjoy receiving a lot of the ball and came close to scoring on several occasions, and the return of Jimmy Greaves after a seven-month absence through jaundice. I cheered heartily when he scored to put England ahead before Bobby Charlton added another to settle the game.

The spectators were relieved, in the end, to see another victory, and somewhat optimistically sent the players off the field with the Liverpool battle cry of 'We're gonna win the cup!' ringing round the stadium. However, in the cold light of the following day the press brought England down with a bump; many, once again, were sceptical about their chances in the World Cup and being openly critical of Ramsey, as he seemed to be continually changing his mind about which players to use and the best system to employ.

Thursday, 26 May 1966 – My Seventeenth Birthday!

Dad had won a couple of bob the previous day betting on a horse called 'Charlottetown' in the Derby, and there was a mood of ambivalence prevailing in the Batchelor household. We all went out to the local Beefeater restaurant as Dad was treating us with his winnings and I felt very sophisticated ordering medium rare steak with all the trimmings. I even had a glass of red wine that I thought tasted disgusting, but it made me feel more of an adult than the pint of shandy that Dad offered.

Mum was beaming and was glad to be dressed up and out of her traditional housecoat that all housewives seemed to wear in those days, she even had her hair done for the occasion. We were joined by my sisters and their boyfriends and Dick, who insisted he wasn't going to eat any 'poncey' food. I received a new Timex watch that I still have to this day although it stopped working long ago.

Football Talk

Even though the tournament was still seven weeks away people were now sporting England football badges and World Cup apparel. We joined in several exchanges with families at adjoining tables who all had an opinion about the prospect of England winning and a thoroughly good time was had by all; although eventually Mum ordered that there be no more talk of 'bloody football'!

Boy to a Man

I felt that as I was nearly eighteen, I was old enough to go into pubs and drink. I had every teenage boy's problem of encountering the usual 'I'm not serving you' reaction, and in truth, I still looked far younger than my seventeen years and had no right to expect to get served. I was sure, though, that I was now a man. I had started to shave every day, although in truth twice a week would have been enough, and had decided to follow boxer Henry Coopers example with Brut aftershave and 'splash it all over'. Cooper still occasionally worked on a fruit and vegetable store he owned in Wembley High Road, and I often spoke to him but tried desperately to keep the worshipful tone from my voice.

"Ello 'Enry, 'ow are yer?' was my typical greeting.

'Better than you,' was his witty reply.

He had been very unlucky to lose recently against Cassius Clay (Mohammed Ali) in a World Championship contest at Highbury when a badly cut eye forced him to retire. He was as keen as anyone to see England do well in the competition and hung Union Jack and St George's flags around his store during the championships.

In fact, as the tournament date loomed closer, many advertising campaigns began to cash in on the World Cup with many stores featuring World Cup products as diverse as World Cup beer and World Cup ties, as well as the obligatory collectable sets of postage stamps and coins.

Summer of Love

Much of the reason for my new-found maturity was the fact that I had fallen in love for the first time with a lovely girl named Penny, who I had met while on a football club tour of Bude in Cornwall at Easter.

I had been playing football for a local team, Kenton Grange since leaving school and was, at first, greatly intimidated by the crudity of local amateur football where the standard of refereeing is so awful that normal rules don't always apply.

Although I was fairly quick and extremely fit at that age, I was also painfully thin and regularly took a battering from opposing centre halves who must have relished the prospect of facing someone so frail. Still, it did help to toughen me up and I enjoyed a good camaraderie with my team-mates, who referred to me as Stevie Wonder, on the rare occasions when I was playing well.

This tour at Easter was memorable for a variety of reasons, many unprintable, but the most memorable of which was pretty Penny. Her parents owned a caravan site and she had her choice of hundreds of free beds at any time of year but I am sure she did not use all of them. Predictably, my brothers thought Penny was cheap, but I thought she was really nice and she certainly helped further my life's education.

We met when, on the advice of an older team mate who seemed very experienced in the art of meeting girls, we went straight to the local Woolworth's store to check out the shop girls. At first I was too shy to speak but after some encouragement from my mates, I eventually asked this very attractive young girl where the best places were in town for a good night out, and to my surprise and delight she invited me to a house party that night. Unfortunately, the distance and the fact she didn't really like football meant our romance was relatively short-lived. We did meet again, however, and exchanged romantic letters for some months and of course I told her, in great detail, about my World Cup experiences. Somehow, I don't think these letters survived much longer than our romance.

FLAMING JUNE

June 1966

England embarked on a pre-tournament tour of Scandinavia on 26 June and easily beat Finland 3–0 with goals from Martin Peters, making his second England appearance, and Roger Hunt, plus a first England goal from Jackie Charlton. This match also marked the debut of Liverpool winger Ian Callaghan.

They then beat Norway 6–1 with Jimmy Greaves again scoring four in a match and John Connelly finding the net alongside a rare England goal by Bobby Moore.

Finally, on 3 July they defeated Denmark 2–0 in Copenhagen, with Jackie Charlton again scoring for England, together with another added by Stoke City's George Eastham.

Ramsey had wisely rotated the team from his squad during this tour and had even given another outing to Ron Springett in addition to a debut for Peter Bonetti, and in so doing was forging a good morale throughout the whole squad. Now, firmly back into winning ways, confidence amongst the England squad was high and the manager was beaming with self-assurance.

England will Win the World Cup

In a television interview, Alf Ramsey repeated his assertion made after the 'Rest of the World' match in 1963 that 'England will win the World Cup' and, of course, every

England football fan in the country believed him devoutly.

The newspapers loved it and splashed his famous quote across every back page headline in the country.

Ramsey spoke in a low monotone with a slightly posh accent, which reflected the elocution lessons he had taken in an attempt to disguise his natural east London 'cockney' speech. Somehow, the accent reflected his aloofness and served to reinforce the view that he had distanced himself from being too close to his players and was certainly well removed from the press and public.

Job Promotion

Back at work, I had recently been promoted from my lowly position as office junior to assist the export director, a task which comprised mainly of filling in export documentation, and to this day I still remember the EFTA declaration form.

I decided my job title should be 'Assistant Export Director' and duly signed my letters as such and this is how this position has appeared on my CV ever since. I also received a massive pay rise to £12 a week, and after some negotiation, Mum agreed to accept my rent contribution as a fiver. As a special treat, I bought her a bottle of Emva cream sherry with my first increased pay packet and actually managed to maintain this tradition for several years afterwards.

Office Games

Meanwhile, in the office it was getting increasingly difficult to concentrate on my job as the excitement over the impending championships mounted.

Amongst my other, less challenging duties, I used to assist the woman in the accounts office by reading out reams of numbers that she punched into a comptometer machine with great speed and dexterity. Of course, this was in the pre-computer age and I was amazed by this device, which resembled a large cash register with dozens of seemingly useless buttons. To liven up proceedings, I used to adopt a football results voice and would interject irrelevant football scores, just to confuse matters. Naturally, my childish behaviour used to annoy this poor woman intensely, but for me it brightened a very dull task.

Elsewhere at work, most of the conversation revolved around the England team selection. 'It's a pity that Jimmy Johnson isn't English as Ramsey couldn't ignore him,' stated our draughtsman, Ken, and we were all inclined to agree.

'Well, he isn't, and if Ramsey still thinks we'll win it then I'm not going to argue,' I added, with far less conviction than I had hoped.

THE FINALS
COUNTDOWN

July at Last

On 5 July England travelled to Chorzow to play their final warm-up game, less than a week before the opening match of the World Championships. There was great controversy about the timing of such a difficult fixture. In a hard fought contest, England managed to beat Poland 1–0 with a goal from Roger Hunt, who had replaced the injured Jimmy Greaves. The match was a dour affair with Poland keen to win and boost their fans after the disappointment at failing to qualify for the finals; the England players were determined not to shirk any tackle for fear of being dropped by Alf Ramsey.

The backbone of England's success was undoubtedly the settled defence, particularly with Gordon Banks in goal. Ramsey tested Peter Bonetti and even recalled Ron Springett on occasion, but there was little doubt over who was the first choice custodian.

With the full-back pairing of Cohen and Wilson working well and Bobby Moore and Jackie Charlton forming the heart of the defence in front of the dependable Gordon Banks, and Nobby Stiles proving the perfect foil for the talents of Bobby Charlton in midfield, Ramsey now had the platform for future success, and all that remained was for some tinkering to be done to some of the midfield and forward places.

A Mood of Optimism

After seven successive victories the public were starting to believe that England could be World Cup winners, and enthusiasm regarding the impending championships started to rise to a fever pitch.

As the tournament opening date loomed, the whole nation seemed to sense that something immense was afoot and every other conversation at every workplace, school and household suddenly had an opinion about England's chances and how difficult it was to get tickets.

Ticket Announcement

'Tickets are like gold dust' was a common expression, and when I heard this from my brother over the tea table one evening I could contain myself no longer.

'How would you like to go to the opening match, Dad?' I asked innocently.

'I'm not paying over the odds to some spiv,' was his terse reply.

'You don't need to, Dad. I've got two tickets and not just for the opening match, but for all of England's group matches and all the other games at Wembley as well, including a quarter-final and a semi-final. I thought you might like to come with me.'

I will always remember his look: a smile of pleasure tinged with a hint of disbelief.

'Have you really got tickets, Stephen?' Mum was the first to speak after a thirty-second, eternal pause. 'Well, you are a clever boy.'

'Yeah, OK, don't overdo it,' I said sheepishly. After all, I was now seventeen!

I then confided to my family how I had secretly sent off

and received my tickets, paid for in full out of my hard-earned wages, and how I wanted my dear old dad to come with me to all the games. Sadly, I had to admit to them that I stood little chance of getting tickets for the final itself, but had put my name forward for a random draw with the FA when registering for tickets. I informed my family that I probably had about a ten million to one chance – as all the old duffers on the FA would surely siphon the winning tickets off to their toffee-nosed chums that had never been to a football match in their lives. My father, who was a taciturn man, agreed with my assessment. Dad had served in the army during the war but rarely spoke of his experiences, and although he had been a tradesman all his life, he possessed an immense knowledge of, seemingly, everything. Usually, when Dad gave his opinion it was as good as a fact and we all believed in his word implicitly. Imagine my horror when he quietly informed me that England wouldn't win. 'The Brazilians are far too good for us and nobody can stop that Pele fellow once he gets going,' he said sagely.

First Doubts

Because Brazil had not been drawn in England's group it hadn't actually occurred to me we could lose to anybody. Suddenly, I began to have my first wavering doubts.

My family disagreed with Dad, and this helped soften the blow. We were unanimous in our opinion that England would win the World Cup – apart from my elder sister, Eleanor, who thought it would be a complete outsider like Peru. As Peru had not even qualified for the championships this comment was treated with derision by all and merely served to fuel our opinion that girls knew nothing about football.

Over the next few hours we began planning the logistics

of what time we would finish work, whether to go by car or the underground, what time we would have our tea and where to meet for the evening games. I then presented my precious book of tickets to my family, who passed them around with awe. I went to bed that night feeling the happiest lad in the world.

World Cup Willie

Finally, World Cup fever infected the whole of England and the FA revealed their mascot for the event, enter... 'World Cup Willie' – a grinning lion wearing a red, white and blue Union Jack football shirt with white football shorts and football boots. 'How daft,' was the opinion of my father, an opinion that was shared by most of the country. Still, it didn't stop me making my own hardboard cut-out World Cup Willie and nailing it to a length of 2 x 1 wood as a 'flag' to carry to the games. In those days, nobody questioned the weaponry potential of a hardboard lion but, on reflection, I suppose it could have inflicted serious damage on any aggressive rival.

I still have a photograph of me standing in my back garden holding my Willie and looking pretty stupid, but you do these things when you are young, especially when suffering from an acute dose of World Cup fever.

World Cup Song

A sadistic record producer decided to profit from the nation's pain by subjecting us to one of the most dreadful records ever made about World Cup Willie being 'World Cup Mad', and of course thousands of gullible people purchased it and every radio station and even *Top of the Pops* featured it incessantly, much to my absolute abhorrence.

A Family Affair

My eldest brother, Len, is seven years older than me and was in the army. As he was on leave during the World Cup, we thought it would be a good idea if he came to some of the games and Dad decided he should alternate his tickets with him.

My younger brother, Dick, was just fifteen and considered too young to go to such important matches; but Dad somehow managed to get two extra tickets for the England versus Mexico match and we were all able to attend this game together.

We also decided to try and go to the other group matches involving teams other than England, as there seemed to be a few tickets to spare at these events.

Office Obsession

The mood of the country was reflected in my place of work, where it soon became known that I had tickets for the competition.

I had always had a keen interest in the office girls at work, especially Jennifer, the blonde and sultry receptionist who had always ignored me to date. Suddenly, I was Mr Popular with everybody as I seemed to be the only person who actually had tickets to attend England's World Cup campaign. I blatantly suggested that I could probably get a ticket to take Jennifer to a match and perhaps we should go out one evening to arrange it. Unfortunately, she was not that desperate to see a World Cup football match and still turned me down.

Let Me See Them

Elsewhere, the guys from the factory shop floor and the office would frequently ask to see my tickets and asked what it felt like to be going – this followed a familiar pattern throughout the tournament. The popular opinion of the tickets was that they were 'nothing special'. I'm not sure what they were expecting football match tickets to look like other than football match tickets. Anyway, this was still a popular attraction and proved to be another distraction from actually doing any work.

Football Team Talk

The lads from the Kenton Grange football team were all envious of me and my new-found status as a live World Cup England supporter, all apart from one other guy I knew who also had a full set of tickets similar to mine.

I still played five-aside football for my team all through the summer on Thursday evenings. I had to inform the manager that I would miss a couple of weeks due to the World Cup. 'I was going to drop you anyway,' was his response, not quite the same as 'How can we possibly manage without you?' which was the reply that I was hoping for. Needless to say, I felt the sacrifice was worth it, as I was determined to see every possible match in the entire tournament.

As a footnote to this, my team did manage to win the summer league without me, although I had played a sufficient number of games to win a medal – just to cap a perfect year.

No Hiding Place

I decided that it was too risky carrying my tickets around with me in my briefcase in case I lost them, and decided to hide them secretly in my bedroom under my mattress. It never occurred to me that my mother would actually look there, as I had also secreted other 'documents' in this hiding place that would have caused great embarrassment if found.

Secret Stash

To my horror, after just a few days the tickets suddenly disappeared. I stripped my bed completely and searched my room extensively; but still no tickets. My dubious magazines were still in place but the envelope containing my tickets had gone. Close to tears, I pleadingly asked my mum if she knew what had happened to them. 'Yes, I found them,' she admitted, 'and I nearly threw them away as they were in a tatty old envelope. And you can get rid of those disgusting magazines,' she ordered, to my cringing humiliation.

'If you mean those *Parade* magazines, they're Len's,' I said cowardly. 'He made me hide them there so you wouldn't know they were his.' Mum then admitted she had mentioned to Len where I had stored my tickets and that he had removed them as a joke. When Len realised how upset I was, he handed them back without fuss but I still told him that I had shopped him to Mum as the owner of my illicit literature as a means of revenge.

Scottish Wit

Amongst the sales reps that were employed at my workplace was a hard-drinking Scotsman, predictably nicknamed 'Jocky' by all the staff, who took great delight in reminding us that Scotland had not lost to England in four years until our lucky win in February and, but for an injustice in their match against Poland, they would have qualified for the finals and given England a run for their money.

'Ye got nae chance,' was his most common expression, and I had to endure this every time he telephoned or called in to the office as soon as he was aware that I would be going to the games.

I was still naive enough to not understand why the whole British nation, including Scotland, Ireland and Wales, were not supporting England. When I suggested to Jocky that he must, in his heart, be hoping for England to win the World Cup he stammered, 'Ye must be joking, sonny! I would rather the bloody Russians won it!'

Disunited Kingdom

I was bemused and ploughed on regardless. 'But we fought wars together,' I said, and, 'I am sure if Scotland were in it and not England we would all be supporting you.'

'How old are you, sonny?' he asked.

'I'm seventeen now,' I said.

'Well, you've got a lot to learn, that's all I can say,' and he walked off, a big man who smoked and sweated profusely, with balding head and a huge protruding stomach. Before leaving the office, he turned his head back and gave me one last parting shot: 'And you've still got nae bloody chance!' He grinned.

I often wondered how he ever became a salesman as he seemed to spend most of his time criticising everybody he had ever met. He had a ribald opinion about every England player that still makes me smile to this day, and his most common was that 'Bobby Moore is just a blondie nancy boy and wouldn't last five minutes in the Scottish League.' He may have been right about Bobby Moore, but I wonder how his political incorrectness survived in these modern times.

Here at Last

Finally, the tournament was upon us and the whole country became World Cup obsessed. Even the Prime Minister took time out to wish 'the boys' all the best and it was impossible to turn on the television or pick up a newspaper without being bombarded with World Cup news and information.

The visiting teams starting arriving and checking into their accommodation in Sunderland, Middlesborough, Birmingham, Liverpool, Manchester and London.

I watched the news avidly as they showed film of the Uruguay team stepping from their team bus at their hotel. The BBC commentator stated: 'Here are the Uruguayans looking fit and muscular,' which I thought was a strange thing to say. I thought they seemed slightly bemused as they stepped from the bus, blinking at the host of camera's facing them and trying to smile and look confident.

Frightened Rabbits

They made me think of how frightened rabbits must look staring at oncoming headlights. I was sure they were terrified at the prospect of facing mighty England at Wembley in the opening match.

'I can't see us losing to that bunch,' stated Dad confidently, and naturally I supported his view. 'At least 3–0,' I predicted, full of self-assurance and feeling more relaxed now I realised the opposition were ordinary human beings after all, despite the fact they were from the other side of the world.

Shake, Rattle and Roll

I still possessed a football rattle I'd had from an early age and found it amongst my assortment of football memorabilia. I even briefly considered repainting it in England colours and taking it to the matches. This device, made of hardwood, comprised a handle and wooden slats in a frame that clicked against a wooden cog when turned by hand. I hadn't used it for years but was pleased to find that it still worked fine. 'You're not taking that bloody thing,' said Dad when he heard me testing it.

'No of course not – I'm just looking at it,' I replied, suddenly embarrassed and realising how stupid the contraption looked. 'Rattles are for babies,' I joked. Yet when I first started going to football in the 1950s most supporters seemed to possess one of these things – not only children. They had been a popular device for a generation but would certainly be considered an offensive weapon nowadays.

I put my old rattle back in the box I used for storing football programmes, old match tickets and newspaper cuttings. I still have the rattle to this day. It still works, making a most irritating racket that invoked great curiosity in my children in years to come, although it hadn't seen the light of day for many years until I unearthed it whilst researching this book. I vaguely recall they may have been used in the First World War as a signalling device, but have never been able to prove this

The Longest Days

I had strategically booked specific England mid-week match days as holiday during the tournament to allow myself preparation and recovery time. I felt I would need all my powers of concentration if I was to be able to help England win. This, in retrospect, was an act of folly as I would then spend the entire day of an evening match just waiting expectantly for the evening to come, by which time my nerves would be shot to pieces. On the Monday of the opening match I was so excited that I awoke about 6 a.m. and was ready to go about twelve hours too early. I wondered if I was the only football fan in history to have become so enraptured by a football match that I was losing all sense of reason. I now know that my emotions at the time and subsequent behaviour are quite common place. I read the *Daily Mirror* from cover to cover and studied the teams for any clue as to the outcome of that evening's momentous event.

Royal Family

Mum wanted to know if I might see the Queen. 'Yes, I expect everyone will see her,' I said sarcastically. 'Do you want me to invite her round for tea?'

'You won't be going anywhere if you talk to me like that,' she responded, and I immediately felt about six years old and actually wondered if she had the power to prevent me going.

'Sorry, Mum,' I quickly added, just in case. She smiled benignly.

'You should have gone to work, you silly bugger,' she said and, as always, she was right.

What to Wear

Deciding what to wear was also a practical difficulty, as I knew Uruguay played in light blue and needed to ensure I wasn't wearing anything in this colour. Was dark blue acceptable?

Once again I was overcome by ridiculous rationale, and as I didn't possess a white jumper, a signal of homosexuality in those days, I opted for jeans, beige pullover and black leather jacket, although Dad still called me a 'scruffy sod' as we left.

THE OPENING MATCH

Monday, 11 July 1966

I had examined my ticket about a thousand times and memorised the entrance as gate 17, turnstile C, east standing enclosure. The price on the ticket was 12s. 6d. (about 62.5p in today's currency) and the plan on the reverse of the ticket gave an informative layout of the stadium, so I had committed to memory the exact location and route I needed to take. I checked to make sure I hadn't mislaid the tickets approximately every five minutes throughout the day and angrily refused my dad's suggestion that he look after both tickets. 'I'm not a kid,' I fumed, patting my pockets desperately as I suddenly couldn't remember if my ticket was now back in my wallet or my back pocket.

Journey's End

By the time we finally set off for Wembley I was a nervous wreck and to make matters worse, Dad had decided to drive the four miles to Wembley. As soon as we got to the end of Fryant Way near to Wembley Park the traffic was at a standstill. I looked at my new watch anxiously, fearing we could spend the next five hours in the biggest traffic jam London had ever seen and completely miss the match.

'I'll have to park here,' he said as we pulled into The Torch pub car park. Dad reluctantly handed over the extortionate two bob parking charge and decided we had time for a pint. 'Shouldn't we go straight in?' I asked, trying to stay calm.

'It's only half past five,' he said. 'Come on, I'll treat you to a pint – you look like you need it.' He smiled.

'I'll have a pint of DD, please,' I requested, and when he emerged from the scrum at the bar a whole ten minutes later I almost snatched the beer from him and proceeded to down the entire pint in approximately 4.2 seconds.

'Now you'll have to wait for me,' he said, lighting a Players No. 6 cigarette and sipping from his pint jug.

'I was thirsty – I don't mind waiting,' I lied, checking my watch yet again.

Last Leg

'Why don't you go and get a couple of programmes?' he suggested, handing me a brown 10 s. note. 'Sure,' I replied hastily, pleased to have something to do that didn't involve just waiting.

I was anxious to get hold of a real World Cup programme and not one of the phoney unofficial World Cup special programmes that had been on sale around London for the last few weeks and had, undoubtedly, conned thousands of tourists.

I stepped into the crowd and immediately drew a response from people regarding my World Cup Willie placard that showed the lion character and bore the simple caption 'England for the Cup'. I bought two programmes, absentmindedly pocketing the 5 s. change, and met Dad as he emerged from the pub.

Finally, we set off to the stadium amidst a throng of flag-waving supporters, in a mood of jingoistic optimism.

A Full Programme

Whilst walking purposefully toward the stadium I was enraptured by the sheer weight of excitement. Everyone around me was an England supporter and it seemed all were smiling and joking optimistically.

Finally we were inside the ground and took up our position on the crash barrier behind one of the goals a whole hour before kick-off and just in time for the opening ceremony.

I avidly studied my 'Jules Rimet World Championship' programme – it hadn't derived the 'World Cup' title to the FA yet, even though this is how everyone referred to it.

The first ten pages were devoted to pen pictures of the FIFA organising committee and comprised a veritable rogue's gallery of twenty or more old farts who all looked as though they had stepped from the FBI most wanted files.

The programme was also littered with cigarette advertising as well as for gin, rum and beer, all claiming to provide health and relaxation benefits to the consumer.

Colour Blindness

The worst programme advertisement of all was a dreadfully politically incorrect panel advertising 'The fabulous Black & White Minstrel Show', featuring 'gorgeous girls and magnificent minstrels'. This seemed woefully dated to me as a young rock fan and the whole ridiculous notion of white men 'blacking up' to sing songs as Negro minstrels is outrageously offensive today but was still very popular with the middle-aged generation of the time.

Who is Number Nineteen?

One unusual aspect of the programme team sheets for me was the numbering of players from one to twenty-two.

England had sensibly lined up with their starting team matching the programme places one to eleven, but Uruguay were playing number fifteen at centre half, number twenty at centre forward and their most renowned player, Hector Silva, at number nineteen.

For every English football fan, this was the first experience of squad numbering and caused some confusion with fans flicking through their programme notes to identify oddly numbered players.

I gazed at page fifty-five of the programme which gave a 2–3–5 line-up, to be filled in by the owner, with the two teams for the final tie at the top, and I willed the England name to be in the top box on the day. This would be match number thirty-two taking place at Wembley Stadium on Saturday, 30 July 1966. Kick-off time 3 p.m.

The Opening Ceremony

The opening of a major World Championship or Olympic Games is celebrated these days with a lavish and spectacular opening ceremony.

To say that England staged a low-key opening ceremony would be the understatement of the century. The entire event lasted just over an hour and comprised of a programme of music and a marching display from various massed military bands.

United Kingdom

For some inexplicable reason, this included the Irish, Welsh and Scots Guards, who must have been thrilled to be a part of the opening tribute to their greatest rival's most historic sporting event. I could only imagine what my friend Jocky would have been thinking of the event. He was watching on television and undoubtedly supporting Uruguay.

The band music was followed by the flag-bearing ceremony, which was composed of a few dozen kids dressed in football uniforms of each of the represented finalists marching around the stadium dog racing track.

Leyton Orientals

The lad at the front of each flag-bearing team held a placard announcing the name of the country he was supposedly representing, followed by another boy carrying their national flag.

To see a toothy, ginger-haired lad representing North Korea seemed pretty funny to me at the time, and the mood of the spectators, by now growing ever more anxious as kick-off approached, was good natured and witty.

The flag parade ended to rousing applause as we waited for the next bout of excitement.

Fanfare for the Common Man

Suddenly, there was an ear-splitting blast from the military bands as they blasted out a fanfare to welcome Her Majesty the Queen. She appeared dressed in a pale blue suit and matching hat, smiling warmly as the crowd clapped and cheered heartedly.

I wondered who had given her such bad advice on her

outfit. Didn't she realise that pale blue was the Uruguay shirt colours – was she secretly supporting the other side? I knew the royal family comprised several nationalities and that Her Majesty travelled the world, but had the Queen ever had a discreet alliance with a Uruguayan? Why else would she be wearing pale blue?

Impatience

I mentioned my observation to my father who looked at me bemused and uttered the immortal words, 'Don't be such a soppy sod,' before returning to studying his *Evening Standard*.

The Queen then proceeded to shake hands with what seemed like just about everybody who wasn't a spectator, much to the rising frustration of the supporters growing impatient for the real business to begin. Once again I checked my watch.

God Save our Team

The crowd hushed completely for a few seconds as the bands broke into the first few chords of *God Save the Queen,* and then virtually everybody in the stadium began to sing with a fervour never experienced before. I have to admit that my own singing was more akin to shouting, as was the bellowing from those around me. Collectively, however, it seemed like a veritable choir. I am certain the last line was cunningly altered to 'God save our *team*' by many of our brethren, though I'm sure Her Majesty didn't notice or mind. As the last bars of the anthem sounded there was a rising cheer from the crowd that swelled to an almighty crescendo as the teams emerged, and I swear, several men around me had tears in their eyes as the moment everyone had been waiting for all these months was upon us.

Finally the tournament was ready to kick-off.

England Line-up

The England team for the opening match was well known and this was confirmed by the squad numbering, although there was still endless speculation about Ramsey having a secret plan.

I liked the look of the team but had my doubts about winger John Connelly. He had enjoyed a good season in the First Division and, for a winger, was a regular goalscorer. I wasn't quite sure why his selection seemed out of place and in the end I put it down to his huge quiff hairstyle, which was, by now, hopelessly dated.

England v Uruguay (Match 1, Group One)

ENGLAND:	Banks, Cohen, Wilson, Stiles, Charlton J, Moore, Ball, Greaves, Charlton R, Hunt, Connelly
URUGUAY:	Mazurkiewicz, Troche, Manicera, Ubinas, Goncalvez, Caetano, Cortes, Viera, Silva, Rocha, Perez
REFEREE:	Isvan Holt (Hungary)
ATTENDANCE:	87,148

The atmosphere on that heady Monday evening was electric as virtually the entire crowd were convinced this was to be a glorious England victory.

I had managed to calm down enough to take in the sur-roundings and felt that everything had taken on an impression of absolute clarity. The floodlights seemed to emphasise the detail on the players' shirts and the grim determination etched on their faces as they prepared for kick-off and I truly felt that I was about to be a witness to history.

However, I was totally confused by the empty spaces at the ground and although it had been well publicised that the stadium could not accommodate the full 100,000 due to the large amount of press and television space needed, it seemed that as many as 10,000 tickets may have been unsold. Dad blamed 'those twits' at the FA and said they were probably expecting 10,000 Uruguayans to turn up, but the vacant spaces certainly didn't detract from the occasion.

This match was my first sight of live South American football and South American footballers, which were rare in Europe and unheard of in England.

Not surprisingly, they didn't look much different from any other football team, but Uruguay did possess a record of being twice winners of this tournament and could not be taken lightly.

Underway at last

From the first whistle England were backed by near hysterical support, which merely served to make the players more edgy and early passes were over hit and tackles mistimed.

Gradually, England started to pick up their play but Uruguay defended resolutely, often keeping ten men behind the ball, and when they broke away, they showed they were capable of playing some fluid football.

They also showed they could be tough and seemed very adept at the more unorthodox ways of preventing opponents making progress, with shirt-pulling being a common method employed.

England become increasingly frustrated, and on the rare

occasions they managed to carve openings in the first half, they found the Uruguayan goalkeeper, Ladislao Mazurkiewicz, more than competent.

The crowd willed England on and very soon adopted *When the Saints Go Marching In* as their World Cup anthem, changing the lyrics to 'When the whites go marching in'. This was sung enthusiastically throughout the opening twenty minutes. However, as the half progressed without an England breakthrough, the mood became more sombre and the spectators groaned as one as repeated attempts at goal was thwarted.

Half-time Talk

Although I was with Dad, we both found ourselves talking to total strangers at half-time, such was the mood of the crowd. It was a curiously social occasion and everyone's spirits were high due to the intoxicating atmosphere.

I can recall a few wise men in our group who actually thought this game would finish as a draw; I remember someone suggesting that the opening matches are always drawn, but I was sure that wasn't true. Still, it did sow the first seeds of doubt as, up until then, the country seemed to be unanimous in expecting an England victory.

Second Half Stalemate

In the second half England enjoyed a spell when they bombarded the Uruguayan goal but every effort was blocked, saved or went narrowly wide.

'We're bound to score soon,' stated my dad wisely.

'Yeah, but when?' I responded anxiously as the time ebbed away. 'Come on England, *come ON!*' I screamed, over and over again, but sadly to no avail.

When the linesman flagged against John Connelly, who was clean through but clearly yards offside, I decided to vent my frustration on him. 'Oi, line-o, can you see anything past that stupid moustache?' I yelled at the top of my voice, to considerable mirth all around. 'What a pillock!' I muttered as I looked at the programme to find out who he was and where he was from. 'Tofik Bakhramov, from bloody Russia,' I announced. 'He obviously knows nothing about football and is probably just here for political reasons,' I deduced. 'Bet nobody will ever have heard of him again after tonight.'

Little did I know that a few weeks later the same Russian linesman would endear himself to the entire English nation and would go down in history as possibly the most famous linesman of all time.

Meanwhile, the tension spread to the crowd, who lapsed into long silent stretches as they concentrated hard on the intrigue unfolding.

With ten minutes remaining the crowd again found voice and a booming chorus of '*England, England!*' reverberated around the ground and the levels of expectancy grew ever higher. If it were possible for will power or lung power to effect the flow of a football it would have been in the back of the Uruguayan net, but the renewed excitement only served to make England play at a more desperate pace and the groans when George Cohen played a wayward forward pass-out for a throw-in were embarrassing.

It's All Over

Suddenly, the final whistle blew; the game was over and with it came the realisation that England had failed to score and win.

It was obvious that Uruguay were very content with the result, as they celebrated wildly at the final whistle, hugging each other, and much to my disgust, some even kissed each other on the cheek in mutual congratulation.

The England fans were stunned and seemed almost reluctant to leave as if, somehow, we might still have another chance to score. Eventually, everyone started to trudge silently home, all slightly bewildered that the match had not gone according to script.

Making his Point

Ramsey was obdurate and considered this the first point won and dismissed any question from the press that this was a disappointing night for England.

He brusquely defended his players and his tactics, arguing that England had most of the possession, were unfortunate in front of goal and praised the Uruguayan goalkeeper for some notable saves – the press were unconvinced.

When Ramsey stated it is difficult, sometimes, to score against teams that are only interested in defending for ninety minutes, some members of the press openly questioned whether England had the players with the capability to prise open well organised defences – perhaps this was merely a taste of what was to come? Ramsey, as usual, brusquely refuted this, stating that he would rate his group of players favourably against those from any other country at this tournament. He then terminated the press conference.

However, despite Ramsey's reluctance to publicly castigate his players, he was already planning to wield the axe for the next match.

Tuesday, 12 July 1966

ELSEWHERE – GROUP STAGES, MATCH 1

Elsewhere, other leading national teams were faring much better than England by recording impressive victories.

West Germany had an emphatic 5–0 win over Switzerland in Group Two after scoring three times in the opening half, with Franz Beckenbauer scoring twice, from his defensive position, and Helmut Haller netting twice from midfield in a match watched by 36,000 at Sheffield Wednesday's Hillsborough ground.

Brazil Nuts

Over 47,000 turned up at Goodison Park, Everton, to witness the Brazilian stars in Group Three, but although they comfortably beat Bulgaria 2–0, with Pele and Garrincha both getting on the score sheet, it was an untidy spectacle marred by some atrocious foul play by Bulgaria and inept refereeing by Herr Tshenscher from West Germany.

Probably the saddest aspect of the whole tournament was the Bulgarians treatment of Pele – unarguably the world's greatest footballer. He was brutally fouled throughout the game, eventually limping off, and was never to show his full repertoire of skills, being a shadow of his former self in subsequent games.

Dad was disgusted. 'Dirty bastards!' was his opinion, as despite everyone's jingoistic view about wanting England to win the World Cup, every football fan in the country, myself included, also wanted to see Pele at his best, and his shameful treatment during this tournament denied both the Brazilian team and the British public.

Russians Might

The USSR easily overcame North Korea at Middlesborough in a match that only drew 23,000 fans in Group Four. The true measure of this performance was not realised until North Korea's subsequent showing.

No Cake Walk

Suddenly, we had a tournament on our hands. The English football-supporting public were forced to realise this was not going to be the walkover we had expected or hoped for.

Having watched England fail to score against Uruguay, all football fans become concerned at how easily the Germans, Russians and Brazilians had found the net and they all seemed to posses the creative type of player that we lacked.

Suddenly the doom mongers were out in force again.

Press Gang

The newspapers were unstinting in their criticism. Although attempting not to appear unpatriotic, they all seemed to suggest that Ramsey was at fault with his tactics and out of touch with the international game. Much of this criticism was due to his attitude to the press, whom he held in scant regard. His aloofness and paternal protectiveness of his players was frustrating to the Fleet Street bloodhounds, and England's comparative failure against Uruguay gave many an opportunity to seek revenge.

When it was announced the England players were to be special guests at Pinewood Studios and would all meet with several celebrated actors, including Sean Connery, prior to the next match, they were roundly condemned as not taking the tournament seriously. Ramsey, however, remained undisturbed, insisting that it was vital players be given an opportunity to relax away from the pressures of the tournament. He insisted the Pinewood event was a pleasant diversion from the intense pressure they were all under.

'Even James Bond couldn't score for England' was a popular headline as the press ridiculed the England team for stargazing instead of training. Some even suggested that Ramsey was doing an 'odd job'. The puns and innuendoes abounded, and a lesser man than Ramsey would have been highly irritated by this unnecessary sniping but, as always, he kept his cool.

Ye Got Nae Bloody Chance!

Back at work I was greeted to the familiar 'Ye got nae bloody chance' phone call from my friend Jocky, who advised me that, 'If ye cannae score against the bloody Uruguayans ye cannae score against nae body.' I tried to explain that if we cannot score against nobody this was in fact a double negative that implied we *could* score against *anybody*. 'Bollocks!' was his succinct response to my attempted grammar lesson. But I have to admit his call unnerved me slightly, as I think the whole country was convinced England would have scored against Uruguay. Simply everyone had an opinion about the match, and according to many people who spoke to me having watched the match on TV, we were denied at least two or three clear-cut penalty kick decisions by dreadful refereeing, none of which I noticed during the game. In retrospect, of course, it seems some form of hysteria had set in as everyone was convinced we should have scored and should have won, yet the scoreline doesn't lie, and in truth, we simply did not play well enough.

All attention now turned to the next match against Mexico and the absolute necessity for England to win.

Team selection was a national obsession and Dad confidently predicted Ramsey would play with two wingers as this was the only way to unlock a stubborn defence. Mexico were certain to be even more defensive than the Uruguayans, as they had shown early in the competition how England could be frustrated.

INTERNATIONAL EVENT

Wednesday, 13 July 1966

FRANCE V MEXICO (GROUP ONE)

FRANCE:	Aubour, Djorkaeff, Artelesa, Buozinski, Bosquier, Bonnell, Gondet, Simon, Herbin, De Bourgoing, Hausser
MEXICO:	Calderon, Chaires, Pena, Nunez, Hernandez, Diaz, Mercado, Reyes, Borja, Fragoso, Padilla
REFEREE:	M Ashenzai (Israel)
ATTENDANCE:	55,000

Everyone's a Comedian

A decent crowd, including Dad, both of my brothers and me, turned up to see a 1–1 draw with most English supporters cheering for the Mexicans.

It was a warm and humid night and I regretted wearing my trusty old leather jacket, which was now too warm for the summer weather.

Ramsey declared after the match that he was highly satisfied by the result and saw nothing to fear from the teams that England had to face in their remaining group matches.

In an uninspiring game, the Mexican team simply looked too small against a robust French side that was well organised but lacked imagination and flair.

The crowd around me were all in good humour again after the deflating experience of Monday night, and it seemed everyone was a wag. 'That French bloke runs funny,' someone bellowed.

'That's because he's got frogs' legs,' followed, and of course we all roared.

Mexican Waves

All the Mexican team were christened 'Pancho' and seemed to sport extravagant hairstyles modelled on Elvis or look like some old western B-movie gunslinger with a thin moustache and mean expression. My favourite was the goalkeeper, Ignacio Calderon, who looked like a Hollywood matinee idol with his black wavy hair and chiselled features. The crowd around me took to him also, and whenever he found himself prostrate after making a save he was greeted to jeers of 'No time for a siesta now, mate!' from one of the crowd.

The dreadful puns continued throughout the game and both teams were treated to generous applause from the good natured audience at the final whistle.

We all trooped off, desperately calculating the various formulas from the Group One results that would ensure England's qualification. We all knew that we badly needed to win the next match, against Mexico, to give ourselves any chance.

'*Hasta la vista*,' I said to my brother later, it being the only Mexican expression I knew.

'Piss off to you too,' he replied.

'Yeah, OK,' I responded, not wishing to pursue this tack any longer.

'I suppose we need to beat Me'hico now,' he said in a vague Spanish accent.

'*Si senor*,' I replied.

'Oh Cisco,' said Dick.

'Oh Pancho,' I responded without thinking.

Sometimes childish images never vanish and the *Cisco Kid* TV programme was probably the only thing we had that remotely related to anything Mexican. Certainly chilli con carne and fajitas were unheard of in England at this time, and the notion of putting a slice of lime into a beer bottle would have got you thrown out of most pubs and working men's clubs of the age.

I then found myself thinking about the French winger and goalscorer on the night, Gerald Hausser, and the damage he could do to England if he were allowed to run at them. He certainly posed a lot of problems for the Mexicans, but they lacked a goalscoring centre forward to take advantage of their intricate build-up play.

Elsewhere

Many of the big guns were still showing England what they could do by recording important first-round victories.

Of them all, Portugal looked the brightest, with Eusebio quick to get off the mark in a 3–1 win over a well-fancied Hungary in Group Three. This was a highly skilled and highly competitive match, which was a benchmark of the standard needed for teams likely to do well in the tournament.

Argentina beat Spain 2–1 in Group Two in a match that shocked many English fans by its brutality and cynicism. Blatant fouls were then followed by angelic apologies to the referee, who simply looked harassed from the start. Spain, no strangers to rough house football themselves, were undone by the sudden burst of flair the Argentineans were more than capable of, and their accomplished centre forward, Luis Artime, scored both goals, with Jose Martinez netting for the Spaniards.

Cool Reception

Italy beat Chile 2–0 in Group Four but were unconvincing. The opinion of most pundits was that Italy possessed many gifted individuals but failed to gel as a team and their infamous defensive wall looked decidedly fragile against a poor Chilean team.

The highlight of a dull match was a fine goal from the excellent Sandro Mazzola, but the crowd of 27,000 was poor for a normally football-mad audience in Sunderland, and the attendance wasn't helped by monsoon weather on the night.

Still, Italy had won their first match to record two vital points, which was something England had failed to do.

I noticed, from my programme, that Italy had to play Russia in their next match, and as I was impressed by how easily the Russians had overcome North Korea, I felt this would be a crunch match from the two teams most likely to qualify from this group.

Thursday, 14 July 1966 – Musical Memories

As this was a World Cup rest day, my younger brother and I decided to get football off our minds by taking in a gig at a local music club, the Fender in Kenton. We had heard that *The Yardbirds* were performing, and although they were still unknown outside London and their records had never disturbed the charts, they were considered a sensational act.

The Yardbirds played rough R & B, in the same genre as the early Rolling Stones, and much talk was of the recent departure of their highly talented young guitarist, Eric 'Slowhand' Clapton and his decision to join John Mayall's Bluesbreakers. 'He must be crazy to leave The Yardbirds,' I stated. 'I bet he'll never be heard of again,' I added in another classic erroneous prophesy. Dick told me they had appointed two new guitarists to replace him: a guy called Jeff Beck and a bloke he had never heard of called Jimmy Page. It was impossible to gauge how talented either guitarist was on the night as the noise was absolutely deafening. From the first chord until the last we were subjected to an audio assault as The Yardbirds performed fast and furious and very, very loud. There were no seats and hundreds of music fans stood shoulder to shoulder in the cramped auditorium, shaking their heads and bodies to the driving beat of the music. I recognised just one song, 'Too Much Monkey Business', as just about everyone shouted along to the chorus. Finally, it was all over and my brother and I staggered out into the street. 'That was great,' I said, sweating profusely.

'What?' said Dick, clearly unable to hear me.

'You're a tosser,' I said, smiling.

'Yeah, well you're a prat,' he replied (or something to that effect – I actually couldn't hear him either).

My ears buzzed as we walked the mile or so home and it was at least an hour before I regained my hearing. We agreed that both of the new guitarists were brilliant and we also felt that The Yardbirds were going to make it big one day. In fact, it was a spin off from The Yardbirds, Led Zeppelin, that made it really big whist The Yardbirds, apart from one top-ten hit, faded into rock folklore.

Friday, 15 July 1966

URUGUAY V FRANCE (GROUP ONE)

URUGUAY: Mazurkiewicz, Troche, Manicera, Ubinas, Goncalvez, Caetano, Cortes, Viera, Silva, Rocha, Perez

FRANCE: Aubour, Djorkaeff, Artelesa, Buozinski, Bosquier, Bonnell, Gondet, Simon, Herbin, De Bourgoing, Hausser

REFEREE: K Galba (Czech)

ATTENDANCE: 40,000

It being the only match played at the White City Stadium in Shepherd's Bush, the entire Batchelor family felt obliged to attend; this was also the spiritual home of Queen's Park Rangers and the closest they would come to any association with the World Cup.

The results from the other Groups meant that England's draw with Uruguay was seen as disappointing and the ideal result for this match would be another 0–0 draw. This was not to be; Uruguay proved what a good team they were by comfortably beating France 2–1 with Cortes and Rocha on the score-sheet, and only a harsh penalty converted by De Bourgoing kept France in the game.

The crowd were separated from the playing pitch by the vast White City greyhound racing track, and this induced an atmosphere of remoteness that seemed to typify the game. The large crowd of around 40,000 had difficulty in finding voice for either team, and most of them had calculated that Uruguay would now top the group and England could not afford to slip up now for fear of an early exit.

The only excitement was the peculiar support given by the English fans to the French as they went in search of an equaliser in the second half, this being the result we all wanted.

Up the Frenchies

We had noticed the quite tuneful manner in which the French supported their side with their *Allez la France* song against Mexico, and a bunch of England supporters attempted to recreate this, much to the amusement of those around. 'Alley le France!' bellowed in a coarse cockney accent doesn't quite have the same tonal qualities, but the support went on unabated. During the second half, the Uruguayans suddenly realised they were winning and opted for their blanket defence, so effective against England, and were treated to an aggressive verbal onslaught from the English support, who felt somehow this tactic was not sporting. Still, they hung on convincingly to record their first win and go to the top of the group.

Elsewhere

Spain recovered from their defeat against Argentina by beating Switzerland 2–1 in Group Two, with goals from Sanchis and Amaro but when compared to the West Germans' 5–0 drubbing of this opposition a few days earlier, this could not be measured as a good performance, and in Middlesborough, North Korea drew 1–1 with Chile in Group Four, watched by a paltry 13,000.

The first big shock of the tournament was in Group Three, played at Everton in front of 51,000 fans, where Hungary beat Brazil 3–1.

The score was level at 1–1 at half-time. The classy Tostao, who had replaced Pele who was out following his injury against Bulgaria, scored for Brazil and Bene netted for the Hungarians. However, the Hungarians also employed some tough tactics during the second half and the Brazilians crumbled when Hungary went 2–1 up through Farkas and when Meszoly put the game out of their reach with a late penalty they looked in disarray and anything but World Champions. This result was greeted with mixed emotions by English fans, who all wanted to see the brilliance of Brazilian football at its best but were pleased to see they were not invincible, and it had not gone unnoticed that they could actually be facing elimination.

MEXICAN STAND-OFF

Saturday, July 16 1966

ENGLAND V MEXICO (GROUP ONE)

ENGLAND:	Banks, Cohen, Wilson, Stiles, Charlton J, Moore, Paine, Greaves, Charlton R, Hunt, Peters
MEXICO:	Calderon, Chaires, Pena, Nunez, Hernandez, Diaz, Mercado, Reyes, Borja, Fragoso, Padilla
REFEREE:	Lo Bello (Italy)
ATTENDANCE:	92,570

England went into this match in fourth place in Group One behind Mexico, due to their solitary goal against France. All supporters now knew that nothing less than a win would suffice if we were to keep our dreams alive.

Alf Ramsey still persisted in the use of a winger by replacing John Connelly with Terry Paine, but also decided to call up Martin Peters instead of Alan Ball.

The support was again rapturous, and *When the Whites Go Marching In* and *England, clap, clap, clap* resonated around the stadium. England started positively but after thirty minutes still hadn't scored, and with Mexico employing similar tactics to the Uruguayans, the players and supporters started to get more than a little apprehensive. Suddenly, the match was not quite as comfortable as expected for England

and it took a quite spectacular goal from Bobby Charlton to break the deadlock.

He gathered the ball in midfield and advanced toward the Mexican goal and, as the defence seemed to part before him, he let fly from twenty-five yards and crashed the ball into the net passed the helpless and bewildered goalkeeper.

The relief at England's first World Cup goal of 1966 was overpowering. The crescendo of applause that followed for the next five minutes bore testimony to the anxieties of the crowd. When they trooped off at half-time with Charlton's superb goal separating the teams, the air was absolutely buzzing, all England fans started talking to one another animatedly about *that* moment. 'What a goal' must have been uttered by all 92,000 fans, as once again smiles and optimism abounded.

England then took control of the match in the second half and simply overrun the Mexicans, who struggled to cope with the urgency of England's play. They swept forward relentlessly, urged on by an enthusiastic and fervent crowd.

'Remember the Alamo!' bellowed one England supporter when Mexico forced a rare corner and we all held our collective breath at the unimaginable prospect of them equalising., Fortunately, Banks held it easily. Then, with fifteen minutes to go, Roger Hunt was on hand to slot the ball home after the Mexican goalkeeper, Calderon, had palmed Greaves' shot straight at his feet to put the result beyond doubt at 2–0.

The crowded again erupted and the remaining minutes were spent singing songs of imminent World Cup glory.

The warmth of human spirit was once again evident as people swapped stories of what club they supported and where they had travelled from. 'Are you going against France?' I was asked.

'I'm going to them all,' I replied proudly, but immediately felt a pang of guilt as I knew I could not get to the final if we made it.

During this evening I met supporters from teams I had only ever read about as they were in a different league to my QPR team. I even had to admit to someone that I had no idea where Aston Villa was and jokingly asked if he was one of the Mexican reserves. This comment inevitably met with stony stares as I seemed to be the only one who found it funny.

Top of the League

By now, everyone had calculated England's position in Group One to be that of leaders with a one goal advantage over Uruguay. As we had drawn against Uruguay who had then beaten France, we were all confident that we would beat France and progress with ease into the quarter-finals.

Talking Point

Bobby Charlton's superlative strike was the talking point all around us and was one of those rare experiences that all football supporters will identify with: when you see it happening in your mind before it actually does. As Charlton honed in on goal the shouts of anticipation from the crowd rose and you knew he was going to let fly. From the moment it left his boot you just absolutely knew it would be a goal.

This was truly one of those moments that I will always treasure and I am sure that many of those around me at the time will have similar memories.

There was much talk of the success of England's team but this was also tinged with some misgivings. Why had we struggled for more than half an hour to break down this rather ordinary team, and in particular, why was Jimmy Greaves not finding the net? Our defensive qualities were in no dispute as we all poured accolades on Gordon Banks, Bobby Moore and their fellow defenders, and our midfield seemed to gel, with Bobby Charlton now in the form of his life; somehow, we lacked penetration up front, as winger Terry Paine had failed to make any impression and seemed the next most likely candidate for Ramsey's tactical changes.

WORLD CUP ROUND-UP

Elsewhere

West Germany drew with Argentina 0–0 in a Group Two match played at Aston Villa, watched by a good crowd of 46,587.

In a bad-tempered and sometimes vicious game the Yugoslavian referee struggled to maintain control and finally sent off the Argentinean defensive midfielder Jorge Albrecht for persistent foul play; although he could have sent off four or five players from each side – such was the level of infringements.

Portugal comfortably beat Bulgaria 3–0 in a Group Three match at Old Trafford, Manchester, with Torres and Eusebio amongst the goalscorers, watched by an enthralled crowd of 25,458.

Bulgaria's blatant foul play was contained by some good refereeing by the Uruguayan Jose Maria Codesal, who was obviously well acquainted with all the dirty tricks from experience of officiating in his own country. The Bulgarians were unable to stop Eusebio in the same manner they had hacked Pele out of their previous game and simply had no answer to the smooth Portuguese style of play.

World Cup Surprise

In the shock of the night, the unfancied USSR beat Italy 1–0 with a second half goal from the talented Igor Chislenko, in Group Four. Italian restaurateurs throughout the country were dismayed as they had high expectations from their team for the tournament, especially after their 2–0 win over Chile.

Italy had made four changes from the previous game, including the omission of star player Giovanni Rivera, and the new line-up failed to click. Only the splendid Sandro Mazzola emerged with credit from the game as he tried, almost single-handedly at times, to take on the stubborn Russian defence. The match was played in typical English summer rain in Sunderland in front of 27,793 supporters. The Italians let their discomfort show as they fumed at the referee and each other as their frustration mounted.

Day of Rest

Football on a Sunday was unheard of during the Sixties, so despite having a potential audience of millions around the world, the World Cup took a rest to allow people to go to church.

Sunday Lunch

At home, in addition to my two brothers we also had two sisters living with us at this time, aged nineteen and twenty-one. Both were attractive girls (for sisters) and, as was traditional in those days, they used to bring prospective suitors around for dinner to 'meet the parents'.

It must be every young girl's nightmare to have two younger, irritating brothers around when they are trying to impress a guy, and in my brother and me they had the worst pairing possible.

Football Knowledge

Apart from the persistent giggling and pointing, Dick and I used to openly ask for money from the poor bloke in order for us to 'get lost'.

This Sunday lunch my sister Esme bought home John, a

very polite and charming young man, who my brother and I childishly christened 'four eyes' because he wore glasses.

I promptly gave him my 'football test' to see if he qualified as a suitable person to be in our house during the World Cup and, to my surprise, he knew all the answers, including the fact that Brian Bedford was the QPR top scorer. Grudgingly, I got to like him, which is just as well because he eventually married Esme and, to date, they have been together for more than forty years.

Table Talk

The lunch table talk was all about England's progress in the Championships. 'They won't beat Argentina,' stated Dad emphatically, but by now I had worked out this was his reverse psychology strategy as he had been hopelessly wrong about every single prediction to date.

Copycat

In order to annoy and embarrass my sister's boyfriends my brother and I had devised a game of imitation. This enterprise involved the simple process of copying exactly what our 'victim' said or did throughout the meal. On this occasion, every time John took a mouthful of food or a drink his actions would be mirrored by Dick and I. 'Is Greaves likely to play?' he enquired of Dad.

'Is Greaves likely to play?' chorused my brother and I.

'Cut it out, you silly sods,' ordered Dad, but by now Dick and I were in fits of laughter as John fumed and my sisters looked exasperated.

Eventually, sanity returned and we all got down to the serious business of discussing England's chances of going all the way and, to his great credit, John took the ribbing in good spirit and seemed to answer, encyclopaedically, all my endless probing regarding the wonderful game of football.

Monday, 18 July 1966

ANOTHER RESPITE

Today was another World Cup rest day, and with no matches being played at all, it provided everyone with some breathing space and an opportunity for the whole country to indulge in the new national obsession of analysing and forecasting the World Cup outcome.

The newspapers had calmed down since England's win over Mexico and were once again uniting behind the manager and the country. World Cup stories and trivia filled the pages and almost every programme on television made some reference to the tournament, with special guests on quiz shows such as the gentleman who had designed 'World Cup Willie' or the Wembley groundsman, who were introduced as celebrities and were generously applauded by everyone who wanted to have some association, no matter how obscure, with the big event.

I Fancy Anyone

Back at work, everyone had selected a different team as their candidates to lift the trophy in case it wasn't England.

I had wisely chosen Portugal, simply because they had beaten Bulgaria so emphatically, but the guys in the office were busy arguing over the merits of Italy, Brazil, Uruguay, Argentina and the new dark horse, Russia. Strangely, no one seemed to mention West Germany, despite their impressive form.

When Jennifer declared innocently, 'I don't know who will win, I fancy them all,' I couldn't help responding with,

'Don't be such a tart, you can't have them all – have me instead!' much to the amusement of all the men in the office.

Jennifer cut me an icy stare and said simply, 'You are such a twat,' before turning on her heels and storming from the room. I wizened and blushed furiously at the put-down but bravely tried to smile through my humiliation.

'Trust a girl not to know,' I murmured, but already I was regretting my retort.

Tuesday, 17 July 1966

PORTUGAL BEAT BRAZIL 3–1 (GROUP THREE)

In the only match played on this day the much vaunted showdown between the world's greatest footballer, Pele, and the new contender, Eusebio, turned into a huge anticlimax.

The match was played at Goodison Park, Everton, and was watched by a huge crowd of 58,479, which was the largest of the tournament for any game not involving England.

Sadly, Pele, who was limping and heavily bandaged before the start and was clearly struggling from injuries sustained against the crude Bulgarians, was finally helped from the pitch when Portuguese defender, Morais, committed the most cynical foul of the tournament to end Pele's and Brazil's participation.

The image of a wincing Pele, leaning heavily on the shoulders of the two Brazilians trainers as he left the pitch, was a grim sight for all lovers of good football.

Brazil Going Loco

Eusebio was twice on the score sheet as Portugal took their place in the quarter-finals with Simoes adding to the total and centre half, Rildo, scoring for Brazil.

Brazil's only hope of qualifying was to pray for a freak

result in the Hungary v Bulgaria match to see if they could squeeze into the next round. The feeling in the country was that most genuine football fans were hoping they could still do it; few believed, however, this would actually happen.

Uruguay v Mexico (Group One)

At the same time that Brazil and Portugal were locked in their epic encounter, my father, both my brothers and myself were once again back at Wembley, this time to witness the two South American teams in England's Group face each other.

This was the final Group One match at Wembley before England's big contest against France, and we went hoping for an innocuous result, such as a 0–0 draw, that may enable England to qualify with only a draw in their next game.

As it happened, this is exactly the result we got, as Mexico looked like a team that had already packed for their summer holidays and were content to sit back and let the opposition come at them. This was a policy totally alien to the Uruguayans.

The crowd of 35,000 hardy souls were notably bored by the proceedings on the pitch and spent much of the evening chanting for England or amusing themselves by singing music hall songs such as *Knees Up Mother Brown* and *Maybe It's Because I'm a Londoner*. Strangely, there was very little audible support for the various league teams and my occasional shout of 'Come on you Rs!' during a quiet moment only met with confused stares.

I had dutifully noted all the scores from previous games in the chart conveniently inserted within the programme and had already calculated the various results England would need to get into the quarter-finals.

Permutations

A win would enable us to qualify top of our group, but any draw would still suffice to get us into the next stage. Even a 1–0 defeat would enable us to finish ahead of France; however, a defeat by 2–0 or more would be disastrous as we would be out of the competition. We couldn't possibly lose by that score, could we?

Suddenly, those nagging doubts started creeping in and I found myself suffering pre-match nerves almost a full twenty-four hours before the game. Everyone around me was singing 'We're gonna win the cup', and here was I with that sinking feeling that we were going to get knocked out.

'Pull yourself together, you twit,' I said to myself.

'What's up with you?' Dad enquired. 'Come on, I want to get home for World Cup Special to see how the others got on,' he said, suddenly walking briskly. I shook off my momentary doubts and hastened after him; after all, I was just as keen to see the highlights of the other matches and realised we only had about half an hour to get home.

Far Eastern Delight

To our utter amazement we got home to discover that the might and wealth of Italy had been humbled by lowly North Korea, who had inflicted a shock 1–0 defeat on the cream of Italian football. A first half goal from that well-known international striker, Pak Doo Ik, had given the Koreans a shock lead. They then defended stoutly for the rest of the match, despite Italy throwing everything at them. The North Koreans were tactically naive but played with spirit and a togetherness that was missing in the Italian team. They fought tigerishly for every ball and the lowly crowd of 17,829 at Middlesborough were immediately transformed into honorary North Koreans as they cheered at every failed attempt on goal by the Italians and roared with delight at the final whistle, knowing they had been witnesses to something truly remarkable. The Italians trooped off looking shell-shocked and demoralised whilst the Koreans celebrated.

Wednesday, 20 July 1966 – The Luckiest Day of my Life

Just when I had given up hope, I received an ordinary looking letter from the FA advising that my name had been successful in the draw to purchase tickets for the World Cup final match and I was to telephone to confirm acceptance and submit payment of 7 s. 6 d. per ticket, plus postage by return.

Quivering with excitement, I immediately called to confirm and wrote a cheque for the required amount, checking several times that I had signed and dated it correctly.

As England were playing this night I had booked the day off work, so I immediately set off for the post office where I sent my ticket request confirmation and cheque by registered mail to ensure it would not get lost in the post.

I couldn't wait to tell Dad and the rest of my family and friends that I had tickets for the World Cup final (even though they hadn't actually arrived yet) and spent the rest of the day in a fit of nerves with the foreboding dread of England being eliminated that night. My over anxious mind then formed the prospect of having tickets for the World Cup final only to be watching the most boring match in history between two unlikely contenders.

Clothes Encounters

It was another warm day and I had to decide what to wear for tonight's match. As I was going with Dad I couldn't be too scruffy, then I realised that I had to wear the same clothes as I had for England's previous match against Mexico as England had won and they were obviously lucky. Perhaps if I wore them to every match England would win the World Cup.

This is football supporter logic at its most superstitious, but I then searched my wardrobe and laundry basket to ensure I had the same outfit from the previous week, finally deciding that the same pants and socks were not essential to bring good fortune.

Elsewhere

In the other matches played the previous night Argentina easily beat Switzerland 2–0. Artime scored again to take his tally to three for the tournament, with the second goal of the game being added by Onega. Argentina were keeping a balanced team with Calics coming in for the suspended Albrecht after his sending off against West Germany. This was their only change in their three matches so far.

Argentina now had five points and had qualified for the next round but could lose the top spot to West Germany on goal difference if they managed to beat Spain, who them- selves had to win to put the Germans out and qualify themselves.

Quarter-final Opposition

It had already been drawn that the winners of Group One would play the second placed team in Group Two so the forthcoming match tonight, featuring West Germany and Spain, took on special significance. However, as this kicked off at the same time as England's match against France, speculation about who would play who in the quarter-finals was put on the back burner until after we had actually managed to qualify.

Anti-French Propaganda

Although allies during the war and nowhere near as overt as the tabloid press today, there existed an awful lot of anti-French feeling going into this game. The French Premier, Charles DeGaul, seemed to be personally responsible for blocking our entry into the new Common Market (EU), and although most British people were against joining anyway, we resented being obstructed by an arrogant Frenchman. The usual joke about 'What have Frenchmen got in common with their mothers – they both have moustaches!' abounded in the lower reaches of the press and spread to every workplace and pub in the country as the match drew nearer.

THE GROUP DECIDER

Wednesday, 20 July 1966

ENGLAND V FRANCE (GROUP ONE)

ENGLAND:	Banks, Cohen, Wilson, Stiles, Charlton J, Moore, Callaghan, Greaves, Charlton R, Hunt, Peters
FRANCE:	Aubour, Djorkaeff, Artelesa, Budzinski, Bosquier, Bonnell, Herbin, Simon, Herbert, Gondet, Hausser
REFEREE:	A Yamasaki (Peru)
ATTENDANCE:	98,270

The only team change from the Mexico match was Ian Callaghan replacing Terry Paine as Alf Ramsey persisted with the use of a recognised winger.

This was my first live experience of a large band of 'foreign' supporters, and I couldn't quite believe the effrontery of the French supporters singing their *Allez la France* song throughout the first half, as this was England's home and somehow I hadn't expected to hear so much 'away' support.

The England supporters responded with the now familiar *When the Whites Go Marching In* anthem and on another evening giddy with excitement and expectation, we urged our heroes on to victory.

The England fans cheered and jeered unsportingly at the French supporters when the French midfielder, Robert

Herbin, was injured early in the game but the roles were reversed moments later, when Jimmy Greaves badly gashed a shin that later needed six stitches and severely reduced his effectiveness during the game.

Roger Hunt scored from close in to give England a one goal lead at half-time, but although clearly the better team, England had failed to dominate in the way the nation had hoped.

Grudge Match

The game was affected by these injuries and more niggling fouls started to creep into the match. The Peruvian referee, Arturo Yamasaki, had his work cut out maintaining discipline.

When Nobby Stiles launched a brutal challenge on France's best player, forward Jacques Simon, which left the player writhing in agony, the whole crowd expected him to blow for a foul and either caution or even send Stiles off, but instead he waved play on and from Greaves' possession the ball was fed to Callaghan from who's cross Roger Hunt bundled in the second and killer goal. The French were incensed but the English fans were delirious and the referee wisely let the goal stand and waved away the French protests. England duly played out the remainder of the game at a stroll, accompanied by a cheerful crowd singing in full voice as qualification was now assured and we were eager for the quarter-finals.

At the final whistle, some French players were still remonstrating with the referee and a voice in my ear yelled, 'Piss off, garlic breath – you're out!' much to the jeers and amusement of those around. The French supporters had long since gone quiet and evaporated from the proceedings, and the England supporters, including myself and Dad, left with beaming smiles and brimming confidence.

England Disgrace

Much to my surprise, the press, whilst heralding another convincing England win, were scathing about the contribution of Nobby Stiles, who had certainly committed more than his fair share of fouls in the match, but was a long way from being as dirty and cynical as many other players in the tournament.

'England's shame' proclaimed one headline, and in the ensuing days this was followed by calls for Ramsey to drop Stiles from the next match as an example of England's commitment to sporting behaviour.

Ramsey Support

Fortunately, Ramsey stood by his man and shrugged off any suggestion of leaving him out, saying he had made an immense contribution to the England play, and preferred instead to focus on the positive aspects of his game – his running and passing – rather than his sometimes overzealous tackling.

When the FA joined in the witch-hunt, with a spokesman suggesting they were concerned that Stiles' behaviour was not conducive to showing a positive image of English football to the world, Ramsey finally snapped that if Stiles had to go he would go too, at which point the subject was promptly dropped. No one doubted he was serious and England's chances of further progress would be reduced to zero without Ramsey at the helm.

Spain's Pain

West Germany beat Spain 2–1 (Group Two) in an exciting match watched by 45,187 at Villa Park.

With the scores level at 1–1 at half-time and both teams in with a chance of qualifying, the German centre forward Uwe Seeler scored what turned out to be the winning goal. Spain finally abandoned their defensive tactics in the final minutes in a desperate search for an equaliser, which made for a terrific and enthralling game for the spectators at the match and for the millions of TV viewers staying up to watch the highlights.

The West Germans emerged as winners of their Group, amassing five points from their three games, with an impressive goal aggregate of seven for and only one against.

Argentina's win the previous day was enough to see them qualify in second place as Spain crashed out and, as England had finished top of Group One, these were to be their next opponents in the quarter-final on the coming Saturday afternoon.

I had already discussed with my brother, Len, arrangements to go by tube to the match, as this could be a rehearsal for the final the following Saturday if we made it through the next game, and the semi-final to be played the following Tuesday evening.

Hungary for Success

In Group Three Hungary beat Bulgaria 3–1 to qualify in second place at the expense of Brazil who, sadly, were eliminated.

Hungary had made an inauspicious entry into the quarter-finals since their opening match defeat by Portugal and had now scored seven goals in their three games with forward Ferenc Bene netting in every match, although they had also conceded five times, suggesting they may be a good attacking team but had defensive frailties.

Red Army

The USSR qualified as winners in Group Four following a 2–1 victory over Chile, who finished bottom of their group with just one point. In this match, played at Sunderland and watched by 16,000 fans, Chile took a surprise lead through midfielder Ruben Marcos only for the Russians to equalise before half-time through left winger Valery Porkujan. The same player scored again in the second half to give the Soviets victory and leave them with a Group summary of played three, won three, scored six with one conceded. However, their excellent goalie, Lev Yashin, had surprisingly made only one appearance in the three matches played and was reported to be carrying a mystery injury. This made it much easier for the press to declare that Gordon Banks was now the best goalkeeper in the world!

Meanwhile, the efficiency of the Russians' progress had not gone unnoticed and many pundits were now tipping them as possible dark horses for the trophy.

Thursday, 21 July 1966

This was a World Cup rest day and for the whole country a return to some form of normality. My office routines had taken on a new form of tedium due to my mental obsession with anything remotely connected to the World Cup.

I felt compelled to read every newspaper and was acutely aware that most dailies were to be found in the works canteen.

Please Ask Me

If a customer phoned up from Birmingham or Liverpool, I immediately knew the results and scorers from any World Cup games played in that city and readily engaged in conversation on that topic, barely waiting for the questions in response that would enable me to declare that I was going to all of England games, including the quarter-final and possibly the semis and final itself. No wonder, then, that my workload was mounting and my boss was becoming increasingly exasperated by my behaviour.

Wee Baldy Guy

When Jocky came on the line to slate England, and Nobby Stiles in particular, I refused to take the bait and kept repeating the fact that we had qualified and were now certain to win the World Cup and he should join in the celebration. He declared that, 'The wee baldy guy should have been sent off, ye must have bribed the referee,' and said he would pull out his own eyes rather than support England – I took it from that he was not likely to change allegiance. 'Argentina are a great side and they could win the whole bloody thing,' he stated confidently, but I sensed that somehow the prospect of England winning the 'whole bloody thing' must have occurred to him, and it clearly rankled.

Friday, 22 July 1966

This was another World Cup rest day and being a Friday meant we all went to the pub after work. Together with a few mates, I decided to make a night of it and go into central London.

I called Mum to notify her I would not be home for dinner and after a couple of pints in the Green Man at Wembley Hill we took the tube from Wembley Central into the big city.

Being summer and the peak of the tourist season meant that the place was packed and, judging by the bunting and posters on display, it seemed that the pubs and restaurants were either totally committed to the World Cup or ignoring it completely.

England Orientals

After trawling through several pubs and being knocked back on numerous attempts to chat up any office girls on a night out, we finished up in Chinatown and opted for a Chinese meal.

The food was memorable but the waiters had to ask us to please keep the noise down as we were disturbing other customers. I couldn't blame him as I was singing *When the Whites Go Marching In* whilst waiting to be served, and this would put anyone off their food. 'It's the World Cup, mate,' I slurred trying to justify my oral outburst, to which he smiled and said, 'Yes, yes, Ingerland will win,' and revealed an England rosette pined to his shirt, to which we all cheered even more raucously.

Tubular Hell

The tube journey home seemed to take all night as we were on the slow train that wanted to stop at every station. Before we were even halfway home, I was busting for a pee but couldn't risk getting off in case there were no more trains. The carriages rang to the occasional burst of World Cup songs interspersed with the usual club rivalry shouts, but in general, it was a peaceful journey and inter-club hostilities seemed to be on some sort of amnesty during the World Cup.

Final Fling

I woke up the following morning nursing an almighty hangover to hear the sound of my mother banging on my bedroom door. 'Come on, get up, you lazy so-and-so,' she insisted. 'There's something for you.' My brain clicked into gear. Something for me – what? breakfast? a parcel? a letter? my World Cup final tickets? Immediately I was awake and tripped over the bed in my haste to pull my jeans on. 'Where's my tee-shirt?' I grumbled as I searched through the heap of clothes on my bedroom floor. Must tidy this up, I thought to myself as I hurried out of the room.

Paternal Generosity

My mum was standing there grinning holding my registered reply from the FA which contained a receipt, a compliment slip and two precious tickets for the 1966 World Cup final!

I couldn't decide whether to laugh or cry, and just stood grinning and gawping at the tickets. 'Does Dad know?' I enquired.

'Yes, but he's gone back to sleep,' Mum replied.

'How can he go back to sleep when it's the quarter-final of the World Cup and I've just got tickets for the final?' I asked incredulously.

'Your dad's not going today, he wants Len to take you,' she explained, much to my surprise.

Finally, over breakfast I quizzed Dad about his decision. 'I said from the start that I would alternate with Len,' he explained. 'If we win today I'll go with you to the semi on Wednesday,' he stated.

'Yeah, but if we win that it'll mean Len'll go to the final instead of you.' I felt a pang of conscience as the heroic thought occurred of offering my World Cup tickets to Dad and Len, and I spluttered this out almost without realising what I said. 'Do you want to take Len to the final with my ticket if we get there?' I asked apprehensively.

'No, of course not, you silly bugger,' he replied, smiling. He was obviously quite aware that was the answer I was hoping for, but seemed pleased I had at least offered.

'Anyway, where is Len?' I asked.

'He stayed round Jackie's last night,' Mum advised, and once again I started looking at the clock and thinking, It's only five hours to kick-off, and we should be ready to go by now. My hangover had vanished but was replaced with the usual anxieties about the day ahead and the immediate problem of what to wear.

ARGENTINE BEEF

Saturday, 23 July 1966

ENGLAND V ARGENTINA (WORLD CUP QUARTER-FINAL)

ENGLAND: Banks, Cohen, Wilson, Stiles, Charlton J, Moore, Ball, Hurst, Charlton R, Hunt, Peters

ARGENTINA: Roma, Perfumo, Marzolini, Ferroiro, Rattin, Albrecht, Solari, Gonzalez, Artime, Onega, Mas

REFEREE: R Krietlein (West Germany)

ATTENDANCE: 90,584

The England changes from the France match were to bring back Alan Ball to replace Ian Callaghan and to call up Geoff Hurst as the replacement for Jimmy Greaves, who had still not recovered from his badly gashed shin. Significantly, Ramsey had finally abandoned the use of a recognised winger altogether and you sensed, somehow, that this was finally *his* team.

Tough Opposition

This was always going to be a tough match against a highly skilled Argentinean team that had enjoyed excellent wins against Spain and Switzerland in addition to a stubborn but impressive 0–0 draw against West Germany. They had conceded only one goal in their three previous games.

They had also displayed a cynicism that had not gone unnoticed and this was referred to by Alf Ramsey when he, rather undiplomatically, said, 'England players must not respond to the Argentines' foul play,' in his pre-match interview on the evening prior to the game.

This created the wrong sort of headlines the next morning and incensed not only the Argentine players but the entire Argentine nation, whose government was to demand an apology for Ramsey's distinct lack of tact and diplomacy.

Brutal Start

Unsurprisingly, the Argentine team more than lived up to their billing and, during a brutal first half-hour that witnessed blatant body-checking, shirt-pulling and deliberate trips and kicks coupled with histrionic dives whenever an Argentine player was fouled, the crowd grew increasingly angry and frustrated.

The shirt-sleeved crowd were both nervous and excited but I was supremely confident before the game that we would win and, having seen Bobby Charlton's performances against Mexico and France, I was convinced we had a world-class player of our own who could turn the game with his vision and explosive finishing.

Temperatures Rising

It was a very hot day and the temperature seemed to have risen several degrees since kick-off. 'They certainly like some argy-bargy,' I quipped, but nobody was smiling as the grim-faced supporters continued to will England on.

The Argentinean captain was a big, strapping guy named Antonio Rattin. Not only was he an uncompromising defender but also a highly talented footballer with excellent ball control and passing ability. Rattin was finally booked, for a trip on Bobby Charlton, as he attempted to reduce the effectiveness of England's playmaker. The fussy West German referee, Rudolph Krietlein, was doing his best to assert his authority on the game against considerable intimidation from the Argentine players and Rattin in particular.

England often threatened but failed to create any clear-cut chances and support started to wane from the booming chanting and singing there had been at the outset.

The supporters were now becoming engrossed in the match that, in our jingoistic eyes, pitted the honest sportsmanship of the English against the ruthless cheating and thuggery of 'Johnny Foreigner'.

Refused to Walk

When Krietlein booked another Argentinean, Luis Artime, for dissent late in the first half, Rattin was incensed and angrily confronted the referee who, to everyone's amazement, suddenly sent him off!

The totally frustrated referee, who must have been struggling to find breath in the hot and humid atmosphere that had seen him blow his whistle a staggering amount of times, had simply had enough of being bullied by Rattin, who had been attempting to boss the game in every way.

All of the England supporters were mightily glad to see the back of him, and not just because it increased our odds of winning if they were reduced to ten men. The fact was, Rattin had also been driving his team and his runs out of defence and astute passes were leaving us severely stretched.

Shockingly, Rattin refused to leave the pitch and continued to confront the referee. A mêlée ensued that saw most of the Argentine bench come onto the field and remonstrate with the referee – even some England players joined the throng, creating a highly charged atmosphere that could have turned very nasty.

Corned Beef

This was somewhat relieved when the crowd took up the rather incongruous chant of 'Corned beef, corned beef, corned beef!' and this rang around the stadium continuously.

I imagined this to be a reference to a recent health scare relating to Argentinean beef, or perhaps it was the only thing the average English football supporter knew about this country.

Regardless of the reasoning, it remains an enduring memory and I joined in enthusiastically.

Somehow, this ridiculous chant relieved the tension and served to relax the crowd, who had been snarling viscously at the Argentine tactics until then, but were now full of good-natured banter and impossibly rude taunts about the opposition's parentage.

Late Stutter

England soon took control of the game in the second half as the Argentines began to look tired and dispirited following the departure of the inspirational Rattin.

However, several half chances went unconverted and the crowd, who had become more jovial since the corned beef taunts, again became concerned that events were not going to plan. When Argentina broke away to fire an attempt just wide of the post, I began to think the inconceivable, that we could lose to ten men in a match that we had dominated. It just wouldn't be fair, would it?

England Through!

When Geoff Hurst headed home Martin Peters' astute cross for England's late second half winner, the relief was immense. After enduring an agonising final ten minutes in which Onega, the Argentinean midfielder, came close to creating an equaliser on two occasions, the noise at the final whistle was thunderous. Suddenly chants of 'We're gonna win the cup!' were starting to ring out, and much of the pre-tournament optimism of Alf Ramsey (and myself) was being shared by many others. 'Animals!' was how Alf Ramsey had contentiously described the Argentinean team after the match, at the end of which he famously refused to allow the England players to swap shirts with the opposition.

Euphoric Atmosphere

The euphoria of the crown spilling onto the Wembley streets for joyous Saturday night celebrations was infectious. Everywhere people were smiling and patting each other on the back in mutual congratulation of England's success.

Cries of 'England, England!' filled the streets and total strangers were embracing each other with joy and a feeling of bonhomie existed all around. I stood for a moment and closed my eyes, trying to savour the moment in my memory. 'Come on, you silly bugger,' disturbed my reverie, as Len urged me to hurry on home.

Saturday Night In

I spent most of the journey home planning a riotous Saturday night out with Len, maybe calling a few mates and going 'up West' (into central London) or just going down The Rest in Kenton, where they had live music and plenty of 'crumpet'.

As it turned out, by the time I'd got home and had dinner I was so exhausted and emotionally drained by the day's events that I had lost the will to go out and wanted only to watch the newsreels and *Match of the Day* highlights, in order to relive the excitement of the match and wallow in the national fervour.

Elsewhere

In the other three quarter-final matches, all being played on this day, there were some outstanding results, although strangely, the match attendances failed to meet earlier turn-outs, due probably to the desire of everyone to watch the England game live on television.

Korean Shockers

After humbling Italy in their previous game, South Korea gave the stylish Portuguese team the fright of their lives by running up a 3–0 lead before succumbing to the brilliance of Eusebio, who netted four goals in an incredible 5–3 victory.

Pak Seung Zin, who had scored in the 1–1 draw with Chile, put South Korea ahead early on before Li Dong Woon and Yang Sung Kook added to the scoreline twice in the opening half-hour before Eusebio and Augusto pulled Portugal back into the game shortly before half-time. Despite a plucky second half display, the South Koreans finally ran out of steam as Eusebio scored twice more, including a penalty after he had been fouled, to put them into the semi-finals against England. It was a truly remarkable match and I remember watching the television enthralled. The 40,000-strong crowd at Everton were treated to a World Cup spectacle of epic proportions, but in the end another David v Goliath finish was not possible.

Blitzkrieg

In the match played at Sheffield Wednesday's Hillsborough stadium over 40,000 fans turned up for an intriguing fixture.

Germany overcame Uruguay with a three-goal second half blitz to run out winners 4–0 as the South Americans were finally compelled to abandon their blanket defence tactics and chase the game. The Germans had scored first through Siggi Held before half-time, but once Beckenbauer had added a second after a stylish run from midfield, the result was never in doubt. The unimaginative Uruguayans surrendered two further goals to Seeler and Haller, as they pushed men forward in an attempt to reduce the deficit, but it was to no avail and in the end, they looked a well-beaten side.

Magyar Misery

The strong but unspectacular USSR team narrowly beat Hungary 2–1, and were now being taken very seriously as possible contenders. A poor attendance of just 20,000 turned up at Sunderland to watch this game, in which Yashin finally proved he was not invincible, but his team were playing with great confidence and were looking a well organised and formidable team. After Igor Chislenko had scored for the USSR and Bene equalised for Hungary, it was left to the hero of the Chile game, winger Valery Porkujan, to score the winner and put Russia into the semi-finals of the World Cup.

Semi-final Line-up

Now all the quarter-final matches were over the nation was left to ponder the outcome of the forthcoming semi-final, which did not bode particularly well for England.

Of the remaining three competing countries it was recognised that Portugal were the side who possessed the most flair and certainly the tournament's best player, Eusebio. However, the fact that they had conceded three goals against lowly South Korea was an omen as it certainly suggested defensive vulnerability.

Sunday, 24 July 1966

WORLD CUP REST DAY

By now the nation was World Cup obsessed and newspapers were running out of good stories to fill the column inches and had been packing the pages with all sorts of football trivia.

Bobby Moore had the good fortune to be married to Tina, a blonde and glamorous ex-model, and her flawless smile appeared in many of the Sunday supplements. In these times, a newspaper wouldn't be so scurrilous as to suggest whether Bobby was receiving his conjugal benefits but there were certainly plenty of references to Ramsey's total ban on late nights and socialising by his players who were pinned down inextricably in their Lilleshall training camp.

Monday, 25 July 1966

At work there was a buzz right through the factory floor when I delivered the morning work production schedules.

The works manager was a jovial chap named Alan Hill, who was the archetypal jolly fat man with his huge girth and red face fixed with an almost permanent smile. Nothing ever bothered Alan and he was a good friend to everyone. Alan wanted to know about my experiences and my impressions of our chances in the semi-finals but had been instructed, by the management, that the World Cup was not to interfere with production schedules; they had even tried to ban World Cup talk on the factory floor with a badly-worded memo.

'Do you think we'll make the final?' he asked surreptitiously, talking out of the side of his mouth.

'Yes, I think we will,' I answered confidently, mimicking his speech style.

'Will you be able to get a ticket, do you think?' he asked, still speaking from the corner of his mouth.

'I've got it,' I grinned manically, 'it arrived on Saturday before the Argie game.'

'You lucky sod!' he said enviously. 'Ssshh, management coming!' he whispered as he spied the managing director approaching.

World Cup Fever

The MD was John Barton, a quiet and polite man who I had privately likened to Alf Ramsey. He was supporting England, but had admitted to me that his family were originally from Scotland. 'Are you from Dumbarton?' I had rather foolishly responded, but fortunately for me he let that comment go unnoticed.

'Do you think we'll make the final?' he asked, much to Alan's astonishment. 'If we do I'll close the factory early on Friday and bring in a few crates of beer for the lads to drink in the conference room upstairs. Is that OK with you, Alan?' he enquired. Strangely, for the first time I can remember, Alan had stopped smiling and was merely looking stunned. 'Er, yes, sure,' he stammered. As the MD sauntered off Alan's face resumed its customary grin and he shook his head and muttered, 'Blimey, that's a turn-up for the books if the old man is going to buy us all beer.'

'It's a pity we can't have a World Cup every month,' I said, suddenly disappointed that I had booked the Friday before the final as holiday and would therefore miss out on a free drink.

Germany Beat Russia

In the first semi-final match played at Goodison Park, Everton, a crowd of 38,273 turned up to witness West Germany beat the USSR 2–1 to win a place in the World Cup final.

Haller put the Germans ahead in the first half before their stylish young defender, Franz Beckenbauer, playing in a new and confusing role as 'sweeper', put them further ahead with a sweetly struck shot in the second half.

The Russians responded well with a fine goal from their most consistent goalscorer, Valerie Porkujan, and in a tense finish in which the Germans also showed a capacity to be ruthless in their tackling, they just managed to hang on for victory.

The German full-back Friedel Lutz had picked up an injury and was hobbling by the end of the game and now looked certain to miss the final.

German Dread

Most of the English nation groaned as we all wanted Russia to win and we now faced up to the reality of an England versus West Germany final, assuming, of course, that we could overcome Portugal and, in particular, the menace of Eusebio.

England Selection Poser

All the talk in the press centred on the England team selection with very few ever guessing correctly. The Jimmy Greaves versus Roger Hunt team selection dilemma was the main talking point at work with most people, me included, in favour of bringing back Greaves, as his nimble footed trickery and knack in front of goal made Hunt look laboured in comparison.

Over the Batchelor dinner table that evening, Dad confidently assured me the Greaves would play, so that was it then.

We all speculated that the Germans would have an extra day to rest and prepare for the final as their match had been played the previous day and wondered whether this would give them any advantage if England got through?

The newspapers and television were now saturated with World Cup stories and it seemed as if this had been building steadily as the tournament progressed.

The pressure on Ramsey and the England players must have been immense. However, they were still resolutely shielded from the media circus at Ramsey's insistence and now no one was prepared to challenge his methods.

PORTUGUESE MEN OF WAR

Tuesday, July 26 1966

ENGLAND V PORTUGAL (WORLD CUP SEMI-FINAL)

ENGLAND: Banks, Cohen, Wilson, Stiles, Charlton J, Moore, Ball, Hurst, Charlton R, Hunt, Peters

PORTUGAL: Periera, Festa, Baptista, Carlos, Conclecao, Graca, Coluna, Augusto, Eusebio, Torres, Simoes

REFEREE: P Schwinte (France)

ATTENDANCE: 94,493

For the first time in the tournament Alf Ramsey picked an unchanged side. His defence had been together throughout the tournament but the use of wingers still haunted him as he was keen to play his new system in which the role of the traditional winger was obsolete.

Ramsey had, so far, tried three separate wingers – Terry Paine, Ian Callaghan and John Connelly – in the championships, but none had impressed and Alf now decided it was time to stick rigidly to his own methods.

The other problem he had to confront was the return to fitness of Jimmy Greaves, whose deft touches and prolific goalscoring feats made it very difficult to ignore him.

The manager finally decided not to risk him for this

game and stuck with his strike force as Geoff Hurst and Roger Hunt.

There was much concern that the gruelling match against Argentina just three days earlier may have taken its toll on the bruised and tired England players.

Ramsey's most significant decision was to appoint Nobby Stiles the task of marking the Portuguese danger man, Eusebio, and thus nullifying the biggest threat to England winning a place in the final.

Ninety Minutes from Glory

What followed was easily the best ninety minutes of the whole tournament. Both teams displayed a propensity to play football as it should be played. The much vaunted hype regarding the potential confrontation between the respective hard men of each team, England's Nobby Stiles and Portugal's Joao Morais, did not materialise as Morais was left out of their team and the contest was played in a true sporting spirit of mutual respect.

It was Portugal who played the most fluent football throughout the early stages and this quelled the enthusiasm of a fervent English crowd still smarting after the ugly confrontation against Argentina.

Banks of England

Despite the greater possession by Portugal and the electric skills of Eusebio, who was shadowed everywhere by his 'minder', Nobby Stiles, few clear chances were being created. England were now looking very solid in defence, with Jackie Charlton outstanding, and they had yet to concede a single goal in the tournament to date. Gordon Banks was in a class of his own and the expression 'as safe as the Banks of England' was the most overused term in the British press.

Ecstatic Moment

Suddenly, after half an hour's play that had seen England being stretched and having to perform at their best to keep the Portuguese at bay, a simple move found Bobby Charlton with a little too much space on the edge of the Portuguese penalty area, from which he fired a crisp shot past the sprawling Periera.

When the ball nestled in the back of the net the crowd seemed to pause and collectively hold its breath before unleashing a torrent of delirium that rumbled into the dark night sky.

'Yes, yes, yes!' screamed the girl in front of me, temporarily deflecting my thoughts from the goal celebrations.

'Were you watching?' asked Dad unnecessarily. 'What a goal!' He smiled.

England Takes Control

If anything, the goal seemed to dampen the spirits of the Portuguese team a little, and thoughts of South Korea's three-goal romp came to mind. England now pushed forward with confidence and threatened to add to their tally on several occasions as the interval approached.

Half-time Sing-song

With the band back on the pitch at half-time the crowd was suddenly in festive mood and a veritable sing-song ensued, with the inevitable choruses of *When the Whites Go Marching In* joined by *Hitler Has Only Got One Ball* to the tune of *Colonel Bogey* as an obvious slur against the Germans, who would provide the opposition in the final. When the fans began a chant of 'We're gonna win the cup!', Dad muttered to me anxiously, 'We haven't won this bloody game yet – don't they know it's bad luck to celebrate too soon?' I was far too busy singing and smiling to believe he could be serious, but then again, we still had another forty-five minutes of Eusebio to contend with, and I took on a more sombre mood as I thought about having to endure the second half if England did not add a second goal soon.

Torres Leads the Way

From the start of the second half it was noticeable that Torres, the tall and elegant Portuguese centre forward, had adopted a much deeper role and this seemed to unsteady Jack Charlton, who wasn't sure whether to follow him deep or mark the space he was leaving. Eusebio also seemed to be changing role and was now appearing in Torres' position as an orthodox centre forward, which in turn gave Nobby Stiles a problem as his man marker. Suddenly Portugal were making problems for us all over the pitch and the confident manner in which England finished the first half disappeared as nerves set in and the opposition realised this was their one big chance for World Cup glory.

Nervous Tension

Twice Eusebio won headers in the penalty area, with Banks saving smartly and Stiles managing to head away another effort.

Still England struggled to impose themselves on the game, which had now developed into an enthralling contest with both teams thoroughly committed to attacking in force and defending with ferocity. The crowd had grown quite silent with the anxiety of the occasion, but as the minutes ticked away they began to find greater and greater voice.

An Absolute Pearler

What followed was one of the greatest goals I have ever seen in my life, absolutely befitting the match and the occasion. With just over ten minutes remaining, Geoff Hurst broke free to the byline and managed to turn the ball back toward the edge of the area where Bobby Charlton was speeding in. Charlton struck the ball with such power and precision that the goalkeeper could hardly move before the net was bulging and the crowd erupted in delight. 'That was a shot like a bloody cannonball!' said Dad, beaming broadly as if even he couldn't believe that Charlton had surpassed his earlier effort. The England team celebrations also seemed to express a huge amount of relief as we now had that vital two-goal gap to separate the teams and give us some breathing space.

'England, England, England!' chanted the crowd in unison as the atmosphere again became charged by an emotional outpouring of national fervour. My throat ached as I shouted as loud as I possibly could as if we all seemed to believe that the volume alone would now carry us through to the final.

Dad still looked concerned. 'It's not over yet, son,' he warned.

We all glanced anxiously at our watches as the match restarted and the countdown began.

Party-pooper

After just three minutes of celebratory mood the crowd were stunned as Torres won a powerful header which Jack Charlton handled on the line and the referee, Pierre Schwinte of France, immediately blew loudly and pointed to the penalty spot. 'No, no!' shouted the spectators in horror as the referee cautioned Charlton but did not send him off.

'Don't worry, Banksy'll save it!' yelled a voice behind me, and suddenly we were all confident again as he had looked unbeatable throughout the tournament and this must unnerve any potential penalty taker.

Of course, it may have unnerved anybody else in the tournament except the one player who had been outstanding throughout: Eusebio. We all held our breath with fingers crossed tightly and muttered private hopes that he wouldn't score as Eusebio took a few paces back before starting his run-up and Banks bounced on the balls of his feet on the line ready to spring into action.

The kick was an anticlimax as Eusebio easily buried the perfect penalty into the bottom left hand corner with Banks hardly moving and Portugal were back in the game with nine minutes now separating England from the World Cup final.

Ten Years in Ten Minutes

I still find it impossible to write about the final ten minutes (the referee added one minute of injury time), as I spent most of the time with my eyes closed, praying silently that we wouldn't throw it away. 'Watch the game,' ordered Dad angrily, but I couldn't bring myself to look, as it seemed every time I did Portugal were attacking and about to score again.

The noise became deafening as the final few minutes arrived and this swelled into a crescendo with each passing second. I felt completely wired and my heart was racing as I fought to control my emotions. 'Come on, England!' I shouted hoarsely, now finally finding the courage to view the proceedings.

Despite Portugal now playing with speed and flair, England defended well, chasing every ball as if their lives depended on it.

We made it! At last the referee blew his whistle and signalled the game was over. The crowd went wild but I watched quietly as the players hugged each other and the opposition in mutual respect. I knew I had witnessed something truly special and felt a pang of regret at the sight of Eusebio trudging off with his face contorted as he cried like a small child.

Nobody wanted to leave the stadium as we shouted endlessly for our heroes to emerge and receive our plaudits but Ramsey had wisely decreed that a lap of honour was premature and instead the players stood and waved at the four sides of the ground from the halfway line and were gone, leaving us no choice but to wend our way home in joyous mood.

Post-match Comment

When the Portuguese manager was asked after the match who he thought would win the World Cup final, he replied, 'You have just seen the World Cup final: England and Portugal were the best two teams in the competition – and England won.' This seemed a little dismissive of West Germany's chances, but certainly endeared him to all England fans and boosted our confidence for the final just a little more.

Night of Wonderment

I couldn't quite believe it – England were through to the World Cup final and I had a ticket! I was fully aware that I was a witness to history in the making.

I lay awake long into the night, running the highlights of the last match through my head and thinking about the final and the endless permutations, which all came to one of only two conclusions: would England win or lose?

My emotions, which had been fraught from the final ten-minute countdown, had finally settled down but my excitement at the enormity of the impending event on Saturday was difficult to control.

Wednesday, 27 July 1966

This was another World Cup rest day but I regretted booking a day's holiday from work as I had no one now to talk to about my experiences of the previous night.

Understanding Boss

I telephoned my boss who graciously agreed that if I could get in by lunchtime he would only count this as a half-day and I took him up on his offer. I duly arrived in the office to a warm welcome from everyone who knew I had been at the game. I recounted my experiences of the match, including the Bobby Charlton spectacular and the nail-biting final ten minutes, to all and sundry for most of the afternoon and was slightly put out when my boss chided me with, 'You're supposed to be here to work.' However, even he had to ask how I felt about going on Saturday and, if I was interested, he knew someone willing to pay up to fifty quid if I knew anywhere I could get my hands on a spare ticket. 'Sorry, no,' I said, not being tempted to sell my brother's ticket and claim I had lost it (or was I?).

I was tempted to call Jocky and gloat over our success but knew he would find a way to put me down, and besides, I was worried about what a glorious time he would have at my expense if we didn't win the final, so decided not to tempt providence.

Gesture of All Gestures

Over dinner during the evening Dad had again reiterated that he would let Len have his ticket for the final, and I couldn't quite understand why he would do this. Len was out at Jackie's again and I told Dad that Len would understand and that he should go now as he was over fifty and England may not get to another World Cup final for a few years yet and Len could always go to the next one we were in. Dad steadfastly refused to be budged and said he was going to watch it in the pub with Bob and Ernie, his brothers, and he was quite happy with that.

Thursday, 28 July 1966

For the World Cup third place play-off match I saw Portugal deservedly beat Russia 2–1 at Wembley and Eusebio take his goal tally to nine to become the tournament's top goalscorer.

Both teams were given warm support from the English fans, who had turned out in good numbers throughout the tournament to make the 1966 event one of the best supported to date.

Contrasting Teams

It was an enthralling match with the flair of the Portuguese being pitted against the solid organisation of the Russians. In the end, it was won by one man's brilliance, the ever consistent Eusebio, who had somehow recovered from his tearful exit at Wembley in the semi-finals against England to treat the world to his full repertoire of skills. Already, he was being hailed as the successor to Pele – the greatest player in the world.

One of the few Englishmen disappointed by England making the finals was the referee for this match, Ken Dagnall, who was one of the nominations to officiate in the final but could not do so now England were playing. He didn't let his disappointment show as he had a fine game and played his part in what was a sportsman-like match. I was pleased to get another chance to watch Lev Yashin in the Russian goal and was not convinced Banks was a better keeper than him.

All in all, it was a satisfactory evening, even though I had to purchase tickets as this game was not included in the multiple match ticket set I had bought before the tournament.

Final Obsession

The only downside to watching this match was that I found it difficult to concentrate due to my obsession with thinking about the final. I worked out whereabouts I would be standing and wondered if I could see the Royal box clearly enough to watch Bobby Moore lift the trophy on Saturday. The World Cup football final was now my all consuming passion.

Friday, 29 July 1966

I awoke around 5 a.m., immediately calculating how many hours were left until kick-off. I then proceeded to get ready for work so I could beat my all-time record for being early.

I had cancelled my day off to take advantage of the free beer at work offer in the afternoon and also wisely realising that I would be going nuts were I to stay at home doing nothing all day. Everyone was amazed to see me at my desk when they arrived and I had actually managed to get some work done at last, as my negligence during the week was catching up with me and customers were starting to complain.

Greetings from Glasgow on the Rhine

Predictably, the phone rang around 9 a.m. with a familiar Scottish voice on the other end. '*Guten tag*,' he said, obviously betraying his allegiance for the match ahead.

'Hi Jocky,' I said. 'Don't tell me, "ye got nae bloody chance",' I mimicked.

'Nae, ye got a chance all right,' he corrected, 'ye got as much chance as a snowball in hell, and I just phoned to say ye should enjoy the time up until kick-off, 'cos it's all going tits-up from then.'

'Thanks, Jocky,' I replied, already regretting the call. 'Is there anything I can do for you work wise, as I'm very busy?' I said tetchily.

'Nae, I just phoned to wind you up,' he said laughing.

I put the phone down and swore loudly, bringing stares from the girls in the office. 'Sorry,' I stammered, blushing. 'Oh, I do hope England win so I can gloat to that fat Scottish twat,' I muttered to myself.

Greaves or Hunt

Most of the talk at work was the speculation about whether Ramsey would pick Roger Hunt or the now fit again Jimmy Greaves to play up front. Few people seemed to realise that Hunt had been Ramsey's first choice striker for years and had a consistently good goalscoring record for Liverpool and England. I thought it was unlikely that Ramsey would drop him now.

THE WORLD CUP
FINAL

Pre-match Nerves

Unsurprisingly for me, England were unchanged again as Ramsey resisted the press clamouring to replace Roger Hunt, who had looked jaded against Portugal, with Jimmy Greaves.

Suitably Attired

It was a typical English summer day, cloudy and muggy, and I couldn't decide what to wear, but for some illogical reason I wanted to be smartly dressed – it was the World Cup final, after all. In the end, I opted for trousers and sports jacket instead of jeans, but couldn't bring myself to wear a suit and tie as suggested by my parents!

The Longest Journey

My brother and I travelled by tube to Wembley Park and were outside the stadium soon after midday. He treated me to a hot dog for lunch and I bought an England rosette in their changed red colours and a new match programme.

Where Did You Get That Hat?

Football souvenir stalls were everywhere but the most enterprising were those selling red and white striped plastic 'boater' hats, as these kept the rain off of your head and the sun out of your eyes whilst making it quite clear which country you supported.

It seemed as if half of all the supporters were wearing this adornment and no one considered how ridiculous they made you look. Of course, my brother and I purchased one each, and despite how flimsy and uncomfortable they were, we proudly marched down Wembley Way with these perched on our heads. I stared in wonderment at the famous Wembley twin towers as we strode purposefully forward. 'Come on, you silly bugger, let's get in before the rush,' he stated impatiently.

Over-exuberance

Everywhere was a sea of red and white as most of the fans had also arrived hours earlier than necessary as if somehow this would make the game start sooner. By 1 p.m. we decided we had better get inside or we may not get a very good position. In those days, you simply stood on the terraces in whatever block was nominated on your ticket. If you were lucky, or early, you got to rest your elbows on the crash barrier. With a full house you barely had elbow room, but somehow you never felt in any danger.

Happy Event

The excitement was immense and everyone around me was cheerful and smiling. I too possessed a manic grin and simply kept thinking to myself, This is a day I'll want to remember all my life, and I was determined to enjoy every second.

Confronting the Enemy

Nothing will ever recapture the scale of expectation and anticipation felt by everyone inside the stadium. I stood, mesmerised, with my brother as we watched and waited for the teams to emerge. We were singing along wildly to whatever song the band were blasting out and interspersing these with various shouts for *Eng-land!* A throng of German supporters to my left were waving a multitude of flags and singing *'Deutschland, Deutschland uber alles!'* which was greeted by jeers from the English. Finally the teams were marching out and the crowd went into raptures.

The national anthems were sung with gusto and mutual respect, and all anyone cared about was for the game to start. England was playing in an unfamiliar red kit as Germany also played in white and had won the toss to decide the colours of the day. The unofficial England anthem had to be hurriedly amended to *When The Reds Go Marching In*.

Saturday, July 30 1966

ENGLAND VERSUS WEST GERMANY (WORLD CUP FINAL)

ENGLAND: Banks, Cohen, Wilson, Stiles, Charlton J, Moore (Captain), Ball, Hurst, Charlton R, Hunt, Peters

GERMANY: Tilkowski, Hottges, Weber, Schulz, Schnellinger, Haller, Beckenbauer, Overath, Seeler (Captain), Held, Emmerich

REFEREE: Gottfried Dienst (Switzerland)

ATTENDANCE: 96,924

First Half: Early Nerves

West Germany kicked off and within ten seconds had committed the first foul of the match from which England built a promising attack and their first shot on goal. Unfortunately, the shooter was Nobby Stiles and his weak effort was easily cleared. 'Shame that wasn't Bobby Charlton,' I said to my brother, 'we could have been one–nil up in the first minute.'

Both teams were guilty of some wayward passing in the early stages, with Germany trying to use the long through ball to target man Seeler to build their attacks. They had their first shot on goal after five minutes as England failed to clear a long ball properly. Siggi Held followed up only to slice his shot hopelessly wide, much to the delight of the English supporters, who jeered in derision.

When Emmerich repeated the same feat a few moments later, troubling the corner flag more than the goal with his effort, the whistles and catcalls of the crowd produced a music hall comedy atmosphere. 'You couldn't hit a barn door with a machine gun!' yelled one spectator as we all laughed nervously.

These misses did at least help ease the tension felt by all.

England Springboard Attacks

The Germans were defending deeply, leaving room for both Charlton and Stiles to make runs from midfield but we couldn't find the final pass. When another long ball was accidentally headed by Jackie Charlton directly into the path of Uwe Seeler, the striker raced through to fire in a shot that was deflected for the first corner kick of the match.

Big Jack made amends with a towering header from Haller's corner that set England up for another attack down the left flank, which culminated with Stiles crossing dangerously, forcing their goalkeeper, Tilkowski, to punch clear under pressure from Hunt. The ball was scooped in again by Charlton and was pinging about in the German penalty area with Tilkowski again punching clear; the pressure was only relieved when referee Klein awarded a free-kick in favour of the goalie, who was now limping and clutching his shoulder.

The crowd had found voice with the excitement of England's pressure and once again, cries of 'England, England!' reverberated around the stadium.

England Take Charge

After ten minutes, another crisp England attack ended with a Martin Peters cross shot that produced the first real save of the match, with Tilkowski diving smartly to his left.

From another long ball, the referee awarded an innocuous free-kick to the Germans that Moore cleared immaculately to prompt yet another English effort culminating again in a Martin Peters shot that this time went narrowly wide. England were seemingly gaining the upper hand, but when the referee awarded yet another West German free-kick, this time for a foul on Seeler by Wilson, he was treated to some ribald abuse by many English supporters. 'Get yer glasses on, ref!' was a common vernacular of the time, and I voiced my own criticisms by shouting, 'Start seeing things both ways, ref!' Other abuse was even more castigating, even questioning his parenthood.

Disaster

From the free-kick the ball was moved across the field, with England having plenty of men back and no immediate signs of danger. Suddenly, out of nowhere, disaster befell England as a seemingly hapless cross from Siggi Held, which would have drifted out harmlessly for a goal kick, was uncharacteristically headed by Ray Wilson directly into the path of Helmut Haller, who promptly steered the ball past Banks' right hand for the opening goal with just thirteen minutes gone.

The English supporters went dumb as the Germans celebrated wildly with seemingly thousands of black, yellow and red flags. However, this was the World Cup final and the urge to encourage our country soon overcame the disappointment as the home fans found their voices and 'England!' chants once again began to ring around the stadium.

Germans on Top

The goal had clearly given West Germany confidence and this was reflected in their passing, which no longer relied on the long punt forward. In contrast, the England passing, and Bobby Charlton's in particular, began to go astray. Nobby Stiles let his frustration show with a clumsy challenge on Beckenbauer, which earned him a verbal ticking off by the referee, much to his disgust.

When Alan Ball was badly fouled by Overath, with a tackle from behind, a few minutes later the crowd were incensed that he was not spoken to.

Equaliser

All English supporters then cheered ironically when the referee blew for a foul as Bobby Moore turned away from Overath with eighteen minutes gone; but before we could yell at the referee for not booking him, Moore had quickly placed the ball and lobbed it into a vacant area on the German six-yard line, into which Geoff Hurst was running to glance a simple header into the net for the England equaliser.

Hats Off to England

The crowd erupted and I hugged my brother and shouted until I was hoarse. For some strange reason, people around me were throwing their new red and white plastic hats into the air in celebration and I did likewise. Unfortunately, I was a little too excited and whereas everyone else managed to catch theirs when they fell mine disappeared several yards behind me never to be seen again. 'Stupid bloody thing anyway,' I muttered in embarrassment.

The relief among the supporters at England's first goal was palpable and the expectation of more goals to come was high. 'Did you know that the team that scores first in the World Cup final always loses?' I uttered loudly. 'And did you know England have never lost a football match to West Germany?' I asserted to my brother and anyone else who wanted to listen.

I wasn't totally sure if either statement was quite correc, but I was certain I had read something similar and badly wanted to boost my confidence and that of those around me.

Dodgy Referee

The crowd cheered again when the referee blew foul a foul on Wilson by Seeler, but this quickly turned openly hostile when he penalised a challenge by Peters on Overath by booking him.

It appeared to most England supporters that the referee was showing a distinct bias toward the Germans and this was becoming increasingly more frustrating.

Sunny England

The sun emerged and beamed brightly as England continued to persevere, but another Bobby Charlton-inspired
move ended disappointingly as Cohen ran into space on the
edge of the penalty area only to scoop the ball hopelessly
wide. Charlton himself managed to get a shot in when
running across the area as he fired a low left foot effort that
sadly did not have enough power and Tilkowski dived to
save comfortably

End to End

The match was now beginning the flow from end to end as
England started to lose their grip and the Germans upped
the tempo, with Beckenbauer becoming far more conspicuous with his runs from deep positions.

Only Banks, moving swiftly off his line to save at the feet
of goalscorer Haller, thwarted a dangerous through ball

England finally won their first corner after nearly half an
hour but it came to nought and then we were surprised to
see Bobby Moore emerge on the edge of the box to fire a
shot high over the bar. The crowd were now enjoying every
moment and the incessant 'Clap, clap, clap, clap, clap
England!' chant continued unabated. By now my throat
ached and my hands were red with the constant clapping,
but I wasn't going to tire as I desperately tried to do my bit
to help my country.

Boo, Hiss!

After yet more poor decisions by referee Dienst, this time
for fouls he saw by Jack Charlton on Emmerich followed by
Hurst, after winning a clean header in their box; and then

Alan Ball being judged to have impeded Held when it was clearly the other way around, the crowd finally gave vent to their fury as angry boos echoed around the stadium.

Absorbing Match

We were immediately drawn back into the fray, and groaning anxiously as a great England move culminated in Geoff Hurst winning a powerful header that hit Tilkowski rather than him save it, Ball latched on to the rebound to fire another effort in but the ball was scrambled away, much to our chagrin.

The West Ham triumvirate of Hurst, Moore and Peters were linking together noticeably and England had cohesion to their play, especially when building attacks on the left flank. However, the West Germans were also becoming more confident when pushing forward.

Sloppy Play

As half-time approached, England suddenly had an attack of the jitters as they lost possession several times in succession to concede a German corner, from which Banks had to produce a stunning double save from Emmerich and Overath. 'Come on, concentrate!' I yelled, as I feared we may concede again and only an immaculate Bobby Moore tackle on Emmerich prevented him having a free run at goal.

The English crowd were now becoming increasingly frustrated, especially when Deinst gave Alan Ball a lecture after another disputed free-kick awarded.

Oo-vay

West Germany's captain and star striker was a short, stocky, balding, thirty-year-old, named Uwe Seeler. (Pronounced

Oo-vay Sailor). He had been part of their West German World Cup winning squad of 1954 as an eighteen-year-old and was idolised by the German fans. 'Oo-vay, Oo-vay!' they chanted in unison whenever he touched the ball. Despite his lack of height he possessed the ability to consistently win balls in the air against much taller defenders, and within a few minutes he twice won far post headers, one of which needed a smart save from Gordon Banks. He also showed he could strike the ball as well with a fierce twenty-five-yard effort that Banks tipped over the bar.

Last Effort

England did manage to close the half on top when prising another clear chance, with the ball falling to Roger Hunt at the edge of the six-yard box. He struck his effort well but the ball rebounded off the goalkeeper and we groaned again as the chance to go in at half-time a goal up had passed.

As the last few minutes ticked away a chorus of *When the Reds Go Marching In* started up and we all sang heartily, realising that although England had not played badly they would need to improve to overcome this resolute German team.

Half-time

During the break, most supporters felt strangely subdued, probably from the sheer emotional effort that had gone into the first intense forty-five minutes. Len and I hardy spoke as we watched the military marching and absorbed the sights and sounds of this wondrous occasion. Within no time the teams were emerging again and immediately a resonant chant of 'England, England!' began and throbbed endlessly as England prepared to restart the match.

Second Half

Without our even noticing, the sun had disappeared and it had started to rain quite heavily. I immediately regretted being minus my stupid hat as the rain plastered my hair to my head.

Within a few minutes we were screaming for a penalty as Charlton sped into the box trying to find an angle for a shot only to be upended, but the hapless referee merely waved play on.

Once again the crowd vented its spleen at the official and this was further exasperated moments later when he whistled handball against Jack Charlton for a ball he claimed that he controlled with his chest on the halfway line.

The pitch was cloying with the heavy rain and players were now slipping and sliding, but in stark contrast, Alan Ball was outstanding with his tireless running and quick passing and England again looked much the stronger team.

A rare slip by Jack Charlton almost left Haller clean through and this served as a warning to England not to throw caution to the wind in pursuit of the wining goal.

Comedy Relief

When Seeler completely mistimed an intended pass and allowed the ball to bobble over his feet for a throw-in, he was roundly jeered by the English fans, one of whom called out, 'Ooh, hello sailor!' in a Dick Emery falsetto voice, to the great amusement of the fans around me.

England Strive For Victory

England continued to press forward, playing much the better football, with Bobby Charlton prominent in every telling England move with his exquisite passing ability in stark contrast to his ridiculous comb over hairstyle, which flopped untidily over his left ear whenever he broke into a sprint.

A crisp England move ended with Peters heading high and wide from a Cohen cross, and although Germany won a series of corners, most of which were squared for Beckenbauer to shoot tamely wide, it was England that were looking most likely to score and the air of expectancy amongst the spectators rose palpably.

Oh My, What a Referee

When Mr Deinst missed an obvious handball by Haller coming out of a German defensive position he again became the subject of crowd abuse, who launched into a chorus of *Oh My, What a Referee* to the tune of *Knees Up Mother Brown*.

Just as this abated, a bad foul on Uwe Seeler by Bobby Moore might have earned a booking but Moore's quick reaction in helping the wounded German to his feet and smiling warmly at the ref helped avoid that confrontation.

It's Looking Good

Banks was looking commanding in the England goal, dealing with a series of hopeful crosses confidently, and in another lightning England break, involving the east London trio, Moore crossed for Hurst to chest down into the path of Peters, who fired narrowly over the bar. With just twenty minutes to go the crowd began to sense that a goal was imminent and the chanting began again in earnest. The main German danger man was Held, who was not afraid to take defenders on and was responsible for most of the

German pressure and virtually all of their corners. Fortunately, Beckenbauer seemed to have left his shooting boots at home and was consistently wayward from these crosses.

Moments of Torment

England continued to pressurise the Germans and when Overath lost possession to Roger Hunt he retaliated with a clumsy foul from which Bobby Moore planted a free-kick invitingly for Jack Charlton to power a header down only to see it bounce just wide. *When the Reds Go Marching In* continued to prompt England to greater efforts.

Another potential penalty appeal was waved away as Hunt looked to be deliberately impeded by Shultz, who guiltily ran away from the incident as Hunt picked himself up protesting.

In complete contrast, Haller's histrionic dive when tripped by Stiles produced an angry response from England players and supporters who were well aware this player was plying his trade in the Italian league where acting and cheating is almost compulsory. To add further insult, a cutting England move involving Ball, Moore, Hurst and Charlton was ended as Charlton was squeezed out between defender and goalkeeper and again looked to have been impeded. Tilkowski then seemed to blatantly feign injury in an attempt to convince the referee that it was he who had been fouled and was duly awarded the free-kick to the total derision of all Englishmen.

The German supporters had began another chant of 'Oo-vay, Oo-vay!' and the English responded with 'England, England!' and this rang around the ground as England again put their foot on the pedal.

Moment of Hope

With just fifteen minutes left, another lightning break saw Bobby Charlton feed Roger Hunt, who squared for Alan Ball who suddenly seemed to have the goal gaping before him and we yelled wildly in hope and expectation. Ball struck his shot forcefully and accurately but a desperate German boot managed to deflect his shot into the side netting for a corner and the crowd's expectation of a goal celebration turned into further demands for success from the resultant corner kick.

Moment of Glory

We did not have to wait long, as from Alan Ball's corner on the right the ball was only partially cleared as far as Geoff Hurst, who then cut into a shooting position from just outside the penalty area. He scuffed his shot as two defenders quickly closed on him, but, inexplicably, the German full-back, Hottges, stuck out a foot and served only to balloon the ball high into the air, falling invitingly for Martin Peters to volley home with aplomb from around six yards out.

The England team celebrated exuberantly, with Gordon Banks running to the halfway line to join in and the crowd was a kaleidoscope of red, white and blue colours dancing in delight amidst a cacophony of sound.

I did not think it was possible to feel so overwhelmingly happy and was smiling, laughing and shouting like a maniac; even my brother, whose military bearing had made him a model of British reserve, was jumping up and down in delight.

All in a Blur

The match restarted in a blur, and as this was the final and we were winning, I was determined not to be such a wimp as I had been in the semi-final when I had my eyes closed for most of the last ten minutes.

When the Reds Go Marching In roared from my side of the ground with the chant of 'England, England!' coming from the other side and a rather bizarre competition ensued with both sides of the ground trying to out-shout each other.

Fortunately, England still seemed committed to attack and Alan Ball went on an exciting run, skipping past two tackles before being abruptly halted by the right full-back, Hottges, who brutally chopped him down.

The free-kick was cleared as Jack Charlton homed in on it but moments later his brother, Bobby, fired wide after a neat pass from Peters as England continued to press.

Last Ten Minutes

By now everyone was continually checking their watches and I was consciously not trying to look for as long as possible. Whenever West Germany attacked we felt our hearts flutter and willed England to keep them at bay. A neat move culminated with Schnellinger firing a fierce twenty-five-yard drive at the England goal that Banks caught contemptuously, to our great delight.

To their credit, England continued to go forward and Geoff Hurst put a difficult header well over the bar to relieve the stress for a few precious seconds.

The crowd, appreciating England's efforts, began a chant of 'We want three!' and they responded with another attack that saw Martin Peters, this time, lift an effort over the bar.

Apart from yet another free-kick awarded against Jack

Charlton, who had got no favours from Mr Dienst all afternoon, the Germans didn't really threaten and the crowd then took up the Liverpool chant, somewhat prematurely, of 'We're gonna win the cup!' By now everyone was in carnival mood, and in a spirit of national pride a chorus of *Rule Britannia* was started and soon spread all the way around the stadium. I couldn't think of one place on earth I would rather be at that moment, furtively glancing down to check my watch, well under the allotted mental time. 'Britain, never, never, never will be slaves!' I bellowed excitedly.

Mr Dienst Does His Best

By now, all England supporters were convinced only the referee could stop us winning the match. He again lectured Stiles after adjudging another foul on Held resulting in a free-kick that Webber headed heart-stoppingly wide from just eight yards. He then followed this by lecturing Banks for alleged time wasting and ruled an offence against Bobby Moore, who reacted angrily, summoning up England's frustration with the official.

'He's a cheat!' I flared at my brother, who rather sportingly suggested he was just doing his best in a difficult job.

Last Five Minutes

The tension was now almost unbearable, especially when the Germans forced another corner kick. The ball was cleared and England again attacked with another flowing move from Moore to Peters to Hunt and then Bobby Charlton, who sadly scuffed his shot wide as he sprinted on to Hunt's lay off.

I noticed how the sun was now shining warmly and felt

this was an omen of good things ahead and decided that if I sang non-stop for the last few minutes the time would pass quicker and I joined in heartily with the choruses all around me.

Last Two Minutes

Another move involving Hurst, Charlton, Peters and Hunt was intercepted, allowing the Germans to break quickly but fortunately Overath shot well wide and we could all relax again.

I have never been able to whistle at high volume but anyone that could was doing so now as we approached the very last minute of the game.

Absolute Agony

The Germans were now reduced to punting long balls forward and we all cheered when Big Jack easily won a header over the back of Seeler some five yards outside our penalty area. Imagine our anguish when the referee blew for another foul at which Charlton angrily dispatched a few course words in his direction, waving his fist in disgust and displeasure.

They couldn't score now, could they? 'Everyone back,' I shouted feebly, as if England may have any other intentions.

Emmerich took the free-kick, driving it straight at England's goal and the ball was deflected off Cohen, to the feet of Held, to the left-hand side of the six-yard box – his shot ricocheted off the standing Haller and span across the open face of the English goal with Banks stranded. As if in slow motion we watched the inevitable outcome as Wolfgang Webber drove the ball into the empty goal and I felt the bile rise in my stomach.

Uncomfortably Numb

As West Germany celebrated scoring this sickening equal-ising goal, the English crowd felt numb, and were silent, in contrast to the few thousand delirious German football fans who were now waving their flags and sounding their klaxons in triumph.

The first reaction from all English supporters was to boo the referee loudly for what was an obviously biased per-formance throughout which had cheated our team, the better team, of victory. But then, I thought the England players might think we were booing them and refrained. 'Banksy was claiming handball,' observed Len, something I had missed completely but which was undoubtedly true, confirming once again my theory that the referee was a closet Nazi.

There was not even time to restart the match before the referee blew for full time and the prospect of a further thirty minutes was now a reality.

Suddenly, from nowhere a shout developed that was taken over by hundreds of people around me. It seemed like an almost childlike reaction against the beastly Germans as if this would somehow avenge the injustice of their last goal: 'We won the war – we won the war!'

This was repeated in unison for several minutes, but I have never heard this in subsequent TV replays and often wonder if this had been dubbed out as being politically offensive.

This retaliatory chant resonated throughout the area where I was standing and brought a sinister chill to the day.

Spiritual Revival

The vociferous support seemed somehow to motivate the players.

I saw Jackie Charlton, who had sunk to his knees at the final whistle, lift his head and physically respond to the crowd; whether it was to this particular chant or just the crowd in general – I will never know. The other players too seemed to react and roll their sleeves up for the next challenge.

British Steel

Suddenly, there was a new steel and determination to the English team, who must have felt cruelly cheated just moments from glory, and were not going to surrender without a fight.

Gradually, the players shook off their dismay and Bobby Moore began prompting and encouraging his team, some of whom had rolled down their socks to lessen the effects of cramp and were sponging themselves with water from a white enamel bucket.

Poltergeist

The Germans, who had been celebrating wildly, were bemused that the cheers of their supporters were completely drowned with this incessant, almost ethnic chant and their supporters, who undoubtedly understood English better than the average Englishman understands German, were incensed and the mood grimly changed from friendly rivalry to outright hostility within a minute as the ghost of the Second World War loomed over the occasion. I sensed the German supporters, even though they had snatched victory from within our grasp in the dying seconds, were simply embarrassed by such a puerile chant and the hostile change of atmosphere and they became strangely quiet.

Extra Time

Having made a quick dash to the toilet, I emerged to see Haller screw a woeful shot wide, just as I feared another German goal.

Cries of 'England, England!' were still resonating and as if to show we, at least, had one player still full of running, Alan Ball picked up a loose ball on the halfway line and went on a direct thirty-yard run to the edge of their box before firing in a dipping drive that Tilkowski was glad to tip over the bar.

Emmerich was finding Cohen highly motivated as he was bundled over for a free-kick and then had a shot blocked by the same player. Bobby and Jack Charlton then combined neatly, with Big Jack appearing on the left wing to float in a teasing cross that was punched from the head of Hurst by the keeper.

The Last Post

Then the moment we all hoped for almost arrived as a Ball corner was worked back to Bobby Charlton on the edge of the area and he sent in a fierce right foot shot, low and hard, that beat the diving goalie only to rebound agonisingly from the post. 'Oh, shit!' I shouted in anger and frustration.

'Shut up, you silly sod, or you'll get us chucked out,' muttered Len.

'Don't be daft,' I responded, but was already checking around to make sure a steward hadn't noticed my misdemeanour.

England continued to press, with Hurst again going close.

The sun was now shining hotter than at any point in the day and I realised I was drenched in sweat, with my shirt sticking to my back in discomfort.

When Held lost possession to Stiles he committed an

ugly foul on the England midfielder that won England a free-kick and the offender a rebuke from the referee, much to the ironic cheers/jeers of the crowd.

The Ball Was In

Then, with ten minutes of extra time gone, came the moment that will be written indelibly into World Cup folklore for all time. An England break on the right found Alan Ball running into space from where he crossed first time to the near post. Hurst was anticipating the pass, which was hit slightly behind him, and, as the crowd roared in expectation, he touched the ball down, allowed it to bounce a couple of times and then swivelled and drove the ball over the goalkeeper's head only to see it cannon off the crossbar and bounce clear. Roger Hunt, who had followed up into the goal, raised his arms in triumph as the ball was then headed clear and the referee loudly blew his whistle.

Confusion then rained for a few seconds as the Germans insisted Mr Dienst consult his linesman, who was flagging from the touchline. Tofik Bakhramov of the USSR then became the hero of the English nation, and the villain of all West Germans, by confirming the ball had crossed the line and was a valid goal.

It Was a Goal!

Although this was scored in the opposite end to where I was standing every Englishman around me was confident the goal would be awarded. The reaction of Roger Hunt who turned instantly with arms aloft was the signal for us all to give judgement to the accuracy of the official's decision, and despite modern scientific analysis and countless video reruns the fact remains – it was a goal!

We Want Four

I joined in the shout of 'We won the war!' again only to realise they were now all shouting 'We want four!' instead. This turned into the assiduous 'Attack, attack – attack, attack, attack!' war cry that indicated the crowd certainly didn't want England to sit on their lead. The half closed without incident and with the call of 'Ramsey, Ramsey!' being taken up by the supporters as he marched onto the pitch to give one last set of instructions to his general, Bobby Moore.

Fifteen Minutes from Triumph

The final segment of this enthralling match started with the West Germans attacking and a dangerous run into the box by Emmerich was thwarted with a timely tackle by George Cohen, who then cleared well under pressure. This was quickly followed by another long-range shot from Beck-enbauer, which was gathered easily by Banks.

An England break gave us hope but Hurst shot weakly at Tilkowski and we gasped a moment later as Held ran clear, only to be flagged offside by our friendly Russian linesman.

The crowd embarked on another rousing chorus of 'Clap, clap, clap, clap, clap, clap, clap, clap, clap – England!' as we all checked our watches for the hundredth time.

We jeered again as Hunt was upended but the referee waved play on and from the break Beckenbauer drilled yet another hopeful shot well wide.

The Run of the Ball

Some of the players were clearly exhausted and reduced to walking pace, whilst Alan Ball seemed tireless and was still chasing everything as if his life depended on it.

Another fine run from Ball fed Cohen overlapping down the right wing, but our cheers turned to moans as his cross sailed woefully over the crossbar with Hunt and Hurst in good positions.

Blitz

Held replied for the Germans with a similar effort high and wide and the same player looked to be clear on goal moments later but was adjudged to have handled, to our great relief. The West Germans were now gaining the upper hand as they pushed for another equaliser and England desperately fought to protect their lead. Held was prominent in everything and headed another effort yards wide from a good position.

From a German corner England broke suddenly and Hunt charged down on goal before unleashing a fierce shot that flew wide of the static Tilkowski. 'Whoooah!' groaned the English crowd in unison, as we were forced to strangle the shouts of 'goal', as the ball whizzed the wrong side of the post.

Mr Bakhramov then earned another huge cheer as he flagged handball against Haller, much to the player's chagrin.

120 Seconds to Go

I was counting the seconds rather than minutes and was terrified at the prospect of another late equaliser. Beckenbauer tried another hopeful forty-yard shot that was easily blocked, and although the Germans had plenty of possession and were working the ball across the field, the English were leaving no space for them to get forward. Then, with one minute left Schnellinger crossed for Haller to head down toward Seeler just six yards from goal. The sigh of relief was immense as the ball was somehow bundled clear and their last chance was gone.

...It Is Now

A German chip into our penalty area was chested down by Moore, who played a one–two with Hunt before hitting a pinpoint forty-yard clearance that found Geoff Hurst galloping into space with the German defence completely out of sight. We screamed at the top of our voices as he bore down on goal before unleashing a thunderbolt shot that nested in the top corner of Tilkowski's goal with the keeper static.

Celebrations

The last thing I can remember about the game was standing behind the goal where Geoff Hurst had scored and as I saw the net bulge I raised my head and my arms to the sky and almost went into total delirium.

The accompanying noise was deafening and I have never heard anything to rival this at any subsequent football match.

I never even noticed that the match did not have time to restart before the referee blew the final whistle, and we wondered for a moment if the goal had actually been awarded. Another huge cheer arose when the manual scoreboard with the large *Radio Times* advert was then changed by a man in white coat to read:

ENGLAND 4, W. GERMANY 2

Everyone was hugging everyone else as total strangers embraced unashamedly and I saw more than one man weeping openly. 'We done it, we done it!' I was babbling hopelessly, not sure whether to laugh or cry. Even my taciturn brother was jumping and shouting with a stupid grin beaming across his face and we hugged each other in delight and triumph.

We shouted Alf Ramsey's name raucously as he was notably conspicuous by his absence as all the players were embracing on the pitch. Bobby Moore then cajoled him and he stepped onto the field to a huge roar and actually smiled for the first time in a month as his hopes, ambitions and predictions had all come true. We then waited impatiently for the cup to be presented.

Illicit Photographs

I suddenly remembered that I had smuggled a camera into the ground with me, and feeling like a criminal I surreptitiously raised it above my head and took some random photographs of people celebrating. I was acutely aware of the 'no photography' notices from the first game and deliberately didn't use my camera during the match for fear of being evicted, but I guessed now that no one would neither notice nor care. I was determined to capture the moments every Englishman had been fantasising about since the tournament began. As it transpired my photographic expertise yielded just four poor quality black and white images in which no detail is apparent. Of course magnification and digital imaging for consumer cameras were still to be invented, but at least my pictures help preserve the memory of the day.

Stairway to Heaven

The crowd continued to shout 'England, England!' over and over again and finally Bobby Moore made his weary way up the steep Wembley steps, pausing to wipe his hands on his shirt before shaking hands with Her Majesty. She was beaming as she presented the trophy and finally he turned to face the supporters and raised the tiny gold statue aloft. Now the whole world knew for sure that England were the World Champions. A beam of sunlight seemed to reflect directly from the trophy as I watched, mesmerised. I was now feeling exhausted from the events of the day. We roundly cheered every England player as he collected his medal and waited for the lap of honour and a chance to see the trophy at a closer distance.

As the players descended the Wembley steps the band suddenly struck up an impromptu rendition of the national anthem, which was sung with huge pride and fervour by all. This was followed by a rousing musical version of *When the Reds Go Marching In,* which was cheerfully accompanied by the sing-along crowd, who now felt the party could begin.

Lap of Honour Dancing

Within a few moments the crowd around me was granted its wish as first Bobby Moore then a succession of players took turns to display the trophy at the delirious fans in their lap of honour. Nobby Stiles performed an impulsive jig in front of us to huge cheers and to our great amusement at seeing this feared hard man perform such a 'girlie' dance.

Final Memory

Finally, there was nothing more to cheer and, with one last glance at the pitch to recapture in my mind's eye the glorious moment, we turned for the exit.

In front of the stadium in those days was a large forecourt up to the main road that led to Wembley High Street in one direction and Wembley Park Station in the other. As

I left the stadium I could see a throng of people by the main road standing several deep waiting for the spectators to emerge. As we approached I realised they were actually applauding us – the spectators!

Broken Willie

Another wave of excitement gripped me, and raising my World Cup Willie high in the air, I ran toward them in triumph. Suddenly disaster struck as the wooden stanchion supporting my symbol of support snapped in two and I found myself holding aloft a two foot lance of broken wood. I turned to retrieve my 'Willie' but already it was being trampled by the crowd behind me and, dropping the remains of the stick, I shrugged and walked on. By now Len had caught me up. 'What happened to your World Cup Willie?' he asked.

'It broke, so I left it,' I replied nonchalantly.

'You should get it back, it might be worth some money one day,' he said sensibly, but I felt it had done its job and had brought me all the luck I needed, although I did take one last glance behind to see where it had fallen. I was surprised to see a middle-aged man had actually picked it up and was carrying it off furtively. 'He's stealing it!' said Len in surprise.

They Couldn't Have Done it Without Us

'Well done, well done,' the people all around us were saying.

'Thanks very much, it's great isn't it?' I responded, feeling they were all obviously directing their compliments at me personally.

'The crowd won it for them,' observed Len as we strode home. 'They were ready to give up when the Jerries scored in the last minute,' he stated. 'It was the crowd that got them going again.'

I pondered his observation. 'So really, I won the World Cup,' I surmised, stretching my powers of logic to the extreme.

'Don't be a twit,' Len responded succinctly and we both smiled at each other at the childish stupidity of our conversation.

Traffic Fanfare

It was about a three-and-a-half-mile walk from Wembley to our house in Kenton and would normally take about an hour. For the entire journey, every car was waving flags and honking their horns – *'Beep, beep, beep, beep, beep, beep, beep, beep, beep – England!'* – everyone shouted the last word even if in mid conversation. There was something surreal about the journey as we were carried along in a wave of euphoria not conscious of the steps we were taking or the surroundings, just red, white and blue and a constant background noise.

Homecoming Heroes

There was an impromptu Batchelor house party as my family welcomed us home as conquerors. Like many households, we had stuck 'Good Luck England' newspaper headlines in our front room window and we went into the street to share our joy with our neighbours as bottles of light ale and stingo were swapped and greetings exchanged. Dad had bought a few of his kin back from the pub and with my Uncle Bob on the piano and my Auntie Babs singing, her ample chest giving testimony to the power of her voice, a true old-fashioned house party was enjoyed by all. After all the shouting I had done my own singing was more Satchmo than Sinatra, but nobody cared.

THE AFTERMATH

Sunday, 31 July 1966

The following morning, despite being allowed to drink several pints of beer the night before, I was awake early and went out to buy the Sunday papers. I bought several different newspapers and they all seemed to have 'Special Edition World Cup Souvenir Issue' labelled across them, and over a cheerful Batchelor breakfast table, we all read avidly of our heroes' performances and religiously scanned all the crowd scene photographs for a glimpse of my brother and I.

'There you are,' said Mum excitedly, pointing at a picture which showed a hundred different faces about the size of a pinhead.

'That could be anybody,' said Dad sensibly, but then declared that Len should be easy to spot as he was head and shoulders taller than anybody else. We never managed to find our picture anywhere and didn't really care as we spent the rest of the morning trying to snatch highlights of the match on the TV newsreels.

'Let's all go to the pub,' said Dad at lunchtime, and we all piled into his treasured Ford Anglia for the mile-long journey to the Beehive pub in Honeypot Lane. The pub was awash with people decked out in red, white and blue and a piano bashed out patriotic songs that everyone was shouting along to. *It's a Long Way to Tipperary* was reaching its noisy climax as we entered and we filed hopefully in behind Dad as he sent Len to the bar to get the drinks in.

Richard and I were restricted to a half of shandy each, but I didn't really mind as I was still feeling the effects of the previous night. Mum was worried about dinner spoiling and stated emphatically that we couldn't stay long as the joint was in the oven, and as always, mother knows best. By the time we'd had a couple of pints and returned home to gorge ourselves on another delicious Sunday roast I was fit for nothing but sleep

The League Cup, 1967

One slightly unpatriotic but highly entertaining episode occurred just six months after the World Cup when watching my beloved Queen's Park Rangers, who by now, with the addition of the mercurial Rodney Marsh, had become an unstoppable force in League Division Three and were also steamrollering their way through to the League Cup Final.

They had drawn with mighty First Division side Leicester City in the third round, who included the prolific goal machine Derek Dougan up front and Gordon Banks in goal. The close proximity of the pitch to the terraces at Loftus Road seemed to unnerve Banks in goal and he had a most uncomfortable night. The QPR fans began a cruel chant of 'Chinaman, Chinaman,' at Banks, presumably as a reference to his hooded eyelids, which gave him a slightly oriental look, and he had possibly the worst game of his illustrious career and was beaten four times as QPR recorded an historic 4–2 win, which included a classic Banks own goal when he carried the ball over his own goal line as it rebounded from the crossbar.

Rangers went on to lift the trophy after coming back from a two-goal deficit to beat West Bromwich Albion in another truly memorable final to win 3–2 and, in the space of just nine months, I had witnessed the two most historic moments of my entire football watching life thus far.

New World Champions

Nine months after England's triumph, in April 1976, came the moment I dreaded.

Scotland became the first country to beat England since the World Cup, winning by 3–2 at Wembley.

Early during the match Jackie Charlton broke a toe but was forced to play on as there were no substitutes in those days. Jimmy Greaves was the only change to the World Cup winning side, playing in place of Roger Hunt, but he too sustained a bad injury that made him a passenger for most of the game.

None of this mattered to the Scots, of course, as they celebrated wildly at the result, and in fairness, they did possess a pretty good side with some wonderfully talented players and had played well on the day.

At precisely 9 a.m. on the following Monday I received the expected call from Jocky. 'Scotland are the World Champions now,' he declared.

'How did you work that out?' I responded.

'easy – England were the champions and we beat ye', so we're now the World Champions. Ye cannae deny it.'

'You poor delusional soul,' I said. 'You actually have to win a tournament to become World Champions, and it's only held every four years. England are the World Champions at least until 1970,' I stated emphatically.

'I think you'll find a few million Scots who will never agree with you on that!' Jocky said, completely oblivious to my reasoning. I realised it was pointless arguing and left him to enjoy his illusion. 'Bye, Jocky, enjoy it while it lasts,' I responded, before terminating the call.

POSTSCRIPT

Many years later I had the good fortune to meet personally with two of the stalwarts of England's historic win – the two Bobbies – Charlton and Moore.

I met Bobby Moore when he was a guest in the board-room of Leyton Orient who were playing Queen's Park Rangers in a Bank Holiday morning kick-off match, which ended as a 0–0 draw. I was invited by a business colleague was also a director of Orient, and he knew I was an avid QPR fan. We enjoyed a magnificent full English breakfast and he then introduced me to Bobby Moore and I shook his hand with pride and awe and muttered a few words that he responded to with his characteristic dimpled smile.

A few years later, I was also fortunate enough to be a business guest at Old Trafford at an evening match that sadly Queen's Park Rangers failed to win. 'Look, there's Bobby Charlton,' said my host, and sure enough I was standing just a few feet from the great man. Despite the fact he was in company and most probably didn't want to be interrupted, I felt compelled to intrude on him for a few seconds, and to his great credit he was the perfect gentle-man and shook my hand and smiled at me warmly when I stuttered the first thing that came into my head – exactly the same words that I had said when I met Bobby Moore a few years previously: 'Er, hello, Bobby. I just want to thank you for giving me one of the greatest moments of my life and to let you know… I was there in '66!'

THE WORLD CUP FINAL MATCH STATISTICS

	ENGLAND			WEST GERMANY		
	90 MIN.	**EXTRA TIME**	**TOTAL**	**90 MIN.**	**EXTRA TIME**	**TOTAL**
GOAL ATTEMPTS						
SHOTS						
Scored	1	2	3	2	0	2
Hit post/bar	0	1	1	0	0	0
Saved	4	2	6	5	1	6
Wide	10	3	13	6	3	9
Blocked	3	1	4	6	4	10
HEADERS						
Scored	1	0	1	0	0	0
Hit post/bar	0	0	0	0	0	0
Saved	1	0	1	1	0	1
Wide	2	0	2	2	1	3
Blocked	0	0	0	0	0	0
TOTAL GOAL ATTEMPTS						
Scored	2	2	4	2	0	2
Hit post/bar	0	1	1	0	0	0
Saved	5	2	7	6	1	7
Wide	12	3	15	8	4	12
Blocked	3	1	4	6	4	10
TOTAL ALL	22	9	31	22	9	31
Corners	3	2	5	5	1	6

FREE-KICKS WON

Fouls	8	3	11	19	1	20
Handball	0	3	3	1	0	1
Offside	1	1	2	0	0	0
TOTAL	9	7	16	20	1	21
Bookings	1	0	1	0	0	0

APPENDIX –
MEMORABILIA

WEST STANDING ENCLOSURE

ENTER AT **H** TURNSTILES

(See plan and conditions on back)

ENTRANCE **57**

EMPIRE STADIUM, WEMBLEY
ASSOCIATION FOOTBALL
INTERNATIONAL MATCH
ENGLAND
v.
REST OF THE WORLD
(F.I.F.A.)
WEDNESDAY, OCTOBER 23rd, 1963
KICK OFF 2-45p.m.

Price 7/6

Chairman,
Wembley Stadium Limited

THIS PORTION TO BE RETAINED
This Ticket is issued on the condition that
it is not re-sold for more than its face value.

England v 'Rest of the World', 23 October 1963

THE FOOTBALL ASSOCIATION
Patron: HER MAJESTY THE QUEEN

Telegraphic Address:
RIMETCUP, LONDON, W.12

Telephone:
SHEPHERDS BUSH 0151

WORLD CUP ORGANISATION
Secretary: DENIS FOLLOWS, M.B.E., B.A.
OLYMPIC ENCLOSURE, WHITE CITY STADIUM, WOOD LANE, LONDON, W.12

Date 12 - 4 - 66.

VOUCHER N° 27866

WORLD CHAMPIONSHIP—JULES RIMET CUP, 1966

Your application for tickets and remittance of £ 7 - 18 - 6 is acknowledged.

We are pleased to advise you that you have been allotted Season Tickets in the following categories in Group:— A .

SEASON	GRADE						£	s.	d.
	1	2	3	4					
10 MATCH					Your Remittance				
6 MATCH			2		Purchase Price of Tickets Allotted Including postage				
					Refund due to you £				
4 MATCH					A cheque for the amount of the refund will be forwarded during the course of the next few days.				
3 MATCH									

The Tickets will be sent to the address on your Application Form after the 1st April, 1966.
Please notify this office of any change of address, quoting application number 351

TO S. J. Batchelor,
22 Repton Road,
Kenton, Harrow,
Middx .

102767.

Authorised by	Refund Voucher No.	Checked by

Booking confirmation

England v Portugal, World Cup Semi-final, 26 July 1966

EMPIRE STADIUM
WEMBLEY

WORLD CHAMPIONSHIP
1966
Jules Rimet Cup
FINAL TIE

D. Follows. SECRETARY.
THE FOOTBALL ASSOCIATION

SATURDAY JULY 30
KICK-OFF 3 p.m.

STANDING
£1-5
(SEE PLAN & CONDITIONS ON BACK)
TO BE RETAINED

ENTER AT
H
TURNSTILES

ENTRANCE
60

WEST
STANDING
ENCLOSURE

England v West Germany, World Cup Final, 30 July 1966

Other World Cup tickets

This page and next: illicit photos taken during the 1966 World Cup Final

Official World Cup programme, 1966

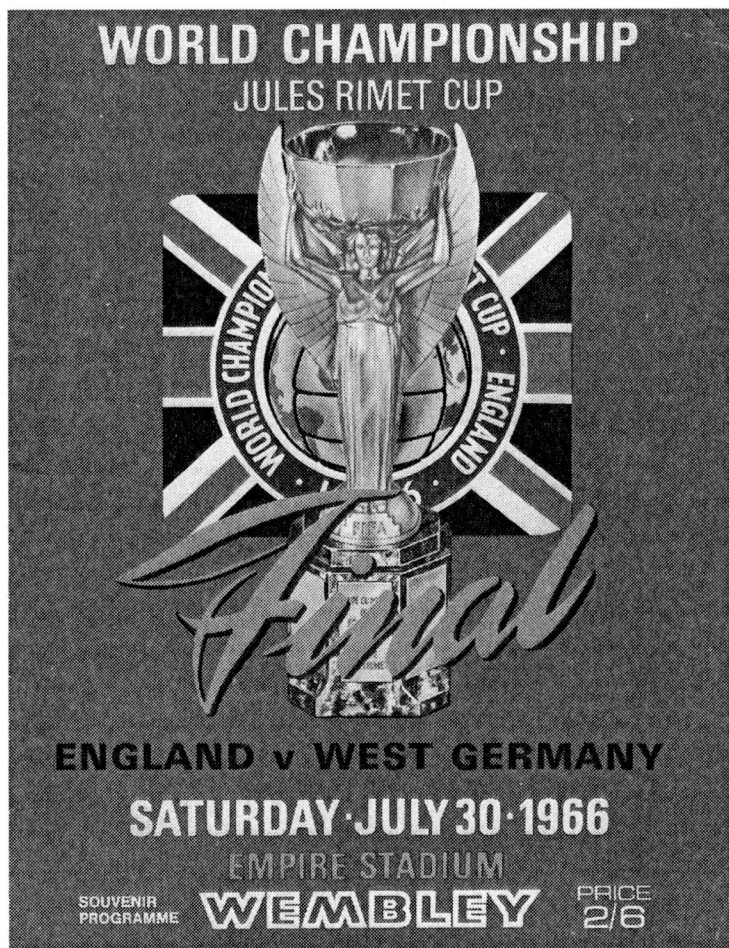

World Cup Final programme, 1966

Rosettes

Printed in the United Kingdom
by Lightning Source UK Ltd.
114210UKS00001B/117